Contents

Foreword

The story of Roy Francis is an emotional tale that will transport you back to pre-and post-war Britain, where the colour of your skin defined you as a person. However, Roy, the illegitimate offspring of an extramarital affair, was not prepared to let the circumstances under which he was conceived nor the colour of his skin define who he was. He stood tall, proud and stoic through all life's challenges. He went on to be a leader of men, white men, during a time when most of wider society would not tolerate his existence.

Roy is without doubt the godfather of modern high-performance sports coaching. To many of his players and supporters, he was seen as a superman but in the end, he, like all of us, was found to be very much human. The insight into this world that Tony Collins paints with words on a page is truly sensational. While reading this book you will believe you are living Roy's life alongside him, getting to understand this great leader and the effect he had on other men.

In rugby league, we like to win, and if it takes a black man to help us do it, then so be it. The spirit of the George Hotel in Huddersfield back in 1895, when good northern principles of fairness and meritocracy helped form the Northern Rugby Football Union, runs through this book alongside the ignorance in those times in equal measure.

The tale of Roy Francis, like rugby league itself, is a human-interest story. At times, the adventures of Roy and his biological father Lionel read like a movie screenplay that will stand the test of time. Like any good story, there are also heroes and villains, and triumphs and tragedies.

Roy Francis: Rugby's Forgotten Black Leader is a captivating read for anyone interested in the plight of the common man, even though Roy Francis himself was no ordinary man.

Martin Offiah MBE
Wigan Warriors
Ambassador

ROY FRANCIS

RUGBY'S
FORGOTTEN
BLACK
LEADER

ROY
FRANCIS

TONY COLLINS

BLOOMSBURY SPORT

LONDON · OXFORD · NEW YORK · NEW DELHI · SYDNEY

BLOOMSBURY SPORT
Bloomsbury Publishing Plc
50 Bedford Square, London, WC1B 3DP, UK
Bloomsbury Publishing Ireland Limited
29 Earlsfort Terrace, Dublin 2, D02 AY28, Ireland

BLOOMSBURY, BLOOMSBURY SPORT and the Diana logo are trademarks of
Bloomsbury Publishing Plc

First published in Great Britain 2025

A catalogue record for this book is available from the British Library

Library of Congress Cataloguing-in-Publication data has been applied for

ISBN: HB: 978-1-3994-1795-2; eBook: 978-1-3994-1796-9

2 4 6 8 10 9 7 5 3 1

Typeset in Adobe Garamond Pro by Deanta Global Publishing Services, Chennai, India
Printed and bound in Great Britain by CPI (Group) UK Ltd, Croydon CR0 4YY

To find out more about our authors and books visit www.bloomsbury.com
and sign up for our newsletters
For product safety related questions contact productsafety@bloomsbury.com

For Jean and John, my parents

Introduction

'Somewhere between what a man does and what a man says,
is what a man is.'

In the 1950s and 1960s one coach dominated rugby like no other: Roy Francis. He led teams to championship wins and Wembley finals, revolutionised the art of coaching, and inspired his players to extraordinary achievements. He introduced film analysis of matches, scientific training techniques, and sports psychology decades before they became commonplace in sport.

But even more amazingly for those times, Roy Francis was a black man leading white players.

In the 1950s, the era of the Notting Hill riots, when signs saying 'no blacks' were commonplace, and when many jobs, organisations and careers were closed to black people, Roy Francis led teams to cup and championship finals.

In 1968, just weeks after Conservative MP Enoch Powell's infamous 'Rivers of Blood' speech, Roy became the first black man ever to coach a team to victory at Wembley Stadium, when his Leeds rugby league side defeated Wakefield Trinity 11-10 in the final second of the most dramatic of all cup finals.

This wasn't the first time a black person had coached a side at the stadium's famous Twin Towers. Nine years earlier, the same Roy Francis had coached the Hull team which lost to Wigan.

Nor was that the first time that a person of colour had coached a professional club to victory in a major British sports final. In 1956 Hull won rugby league's championship final, coached by the very same Roy Francis.

Black achievement in rugby league was not unusual. As far back as 1947 the sport selected the first-ever black athlete to play for Great Britain in either code of rugby. The name of that pioneering player? None other than Roy Francis.

Sadly, in spite of this unique record of achievement, innovation, and leadership, Roy Francis' story has been almost forgotten or remained unknown over the past 50 years.

Yet Roy's story has an even greater significance beyond sport. He grew up in the 1920s and 1930s, part of Britain's pre-Windrush black community. Roy's grandfather arrived in Wales in the 1880s, while his father came from Trinidad to work as a coal-miner in the Welsh valleys. His family was one of hundreds who worked in the mines, steelworks and dockyards across Britain, and his experiences mirrored those of thousands of other working-class black Britons whose stories and contributions have rarely been acknowledged.

His life is not only one of the great lost stories of black British achievement, it is also a record of the obstacles that his generation faced.

As he sought to make the most of his considerable talents, he faced overt racism, subtle discrimination, and, occasionally, open violence. The wounds suffered by his parents were still a raw inheritance for him and, regardless of his success, were always present for him.

While his father fought racism through political action, Roy used his sporting success to try to create an environment free of prejudice. When he left Welsh rugby union to play rugby league in the north of England, he found a sport that gave black athletes greater opportunities than any other sport at that time. Indeed, as this book explains, he was one of many great black players who from the 1930s found a welcome in rugby league. But, as he would discover at the peak of his coaching career, even this was not enough to protect him from bigotry. His inability to escape society's racism would haunt him throughout his life.

Despite these struggles, he became an inspirational figure to those he coached and those who supported his teams. He was a guide, a mentor and a surrogate father not only to dozens of young players but also to their wives and girlfriends. Few sports coaches have left such a personal legacy for those they led.

Like most people of working-class origin, Roy left no diaries, letters, or other written records, and his life today resides largely in the memories of those who knew him. We are lucky that he achieved fame as a rugby player and coach, which has allowed me to reconstruct some of his life story from press reports and interviews. His family history is much more obscure and has been discoverable to a limited extent only through long hours searching in archives and a considerable amount of luck. It is thanks to the memories of his two sons, Geoff and Ian, their wives, Anne and Jean, and the many players and officials who knew him that I have been able to begin to appreciate the complexity of the man and his personality. Roy emphasised the importance of character to his players by saying 'somewhere between what a man does and what a man says, is what a man is', and this has been a useful guide for his biographer too.

To those whose memories of the man still remain vivid, we should be grateful. Roy Francis was a remarkable man who achieved extraordinary things in difficult and sometimes dark circumstances. It has taken too long to rescue his story from fading memories, sporting obscurity, and a wilful ignorance of the long history of black working-class people in Britain. Roy Francis was a hero to many of those who knew and followed him, and he stands as a beacon for those future generations who never knew him but will be able to equal and surpass the achievements of British sport's great forgotten black leader.

1

From The Black Atlantic to Brynmawr: 1919–1936

'I am not willing to suffer when I am innocent.'

Roy Francis was born at 57 Tudor Street, Cardiff on 20 January, 1919.

His father was Albert Francies, a black merchant seaman, and his mother was a white Welsh woman called Alice May Francies. Although they were married, Roy's father lived in Ebbw Vale and his mother in Cardiff.

Or so it says on Roy's birth certificate.

In fact, almost none of those details appear to be correct. Roy's name was Francis, not Francies. Neither Albert Francies nor Alice May Francies can be found on any other official documents of the time. No marriage certificate for the couple exists. There is no record of an Albert Francies ever living in Ebbw Vale, while the address given by Alice May Francies was not hers but that of 'Nurse Cleverley's Maternity Nursing Home' in Cardiff, where she gave birth to baby Roy.

To add to the mystery, the 1921 Census stated that the whereabouts of Roy's parents was 'Not Known' and gives his place of birth as Port Talbot. And on his own marriage certificate in 1939, Roy stated that his father was an evangelist called Anthony Hugh Francis.

The circumstances of Roy's birth remain a puzzle to his descendants even today. Family folklore has it that Albert was the husband of Rebecca Francis, a mixed-race Welsh woman who adopted and raised Roy, and that the baby was the result of Albert's extra-marital affair with another woman. But Rebecca's husband was called Lionel, not Albert, and he and Rebecca lived in Brynmawr, some 30 miles from Cardiff.

Apart from his date and place of birth, the only thing we know with certainty is that the infant Roy was adopted by Rebecca Francis at some point between his birth and summer 1921. The Census of June 1921 recorded him as living with Rebecca and her 14-year-old daughter Olive at 205 King Street, Brynmawr. The rest is a mystery.

So who was Roy Francis?

A CHILD OF THE BLACK ATLANTIC

In fact, Roy was the son of 19-year-old Alice May Evans, the unmarried daughter of a farmer in Brynmawr, and Lionel Francis, a 37-year-old Trinidad-born miner and preacher who lived at King Street in Brynmawr. Lionel was already married, and Alice had gone to Nurse Cleverly's maternity home in Cardiff because it was close to the multiracial dockland area of Tiger Bay, where a mixed-race baby would not raise eyebrows.

Lionel was well-known in Brynmawr. He worked as a miner but had made a name for himself as a charismatic local preacher. He and his wife Rebecca had been married since 1906 and had an 11-year-old daughter, Olive. She was not the only child he had fathered. In 1901 Rose Dibbin, the wife of the family he was lodging with in nearby Blaina, gave birth to a son, Arthur. The boy was not her husband's, but Lionel's. Arthur Dibbins' paternity was well-known, and Roy was raised with the knowledge that Arthur was his half-brother.

Handsome, charming and clever, Lionel was born Lionel Anthony Francis in 1881 in Port of Spain, the capital of Trinidad. Other than the fact that his father Simeon was a blacksmith on the island, nothing else is known about his early life or his family history. Nor do we know when or how he arrived in Wales. The recorded account of Lionel's life begins with the Census of 1901, which lists him as working as a labourer in Blaina. After the birth of his illegitimate son, Arthur Dibbin, in 1901 Lionel decamped to Brynmawr and in 1904 he was working as a deputy check-weigher in a local coal mine.

In those days, Welsh miners were usually paid according to the weight of the coal they dug, as calculated by the mine-owner's 'weighman'. To prevent the company under-weighing the coal and not paying the correct wages, miners would elect check-weighers to make sure that coal was properly weighed. Only those miners trusted by their workmates were elected to check-weighing positions. The fact that Lionel, a black man in his early 20s, was elected to such a position of authority shows the esteem in which he must have been held by an almost entirely white workforce.

Lionel was one of 50 black miners in South Wales in the 1900s. Working side-by-side in the bowels of the earth showed many colliers that skin colour had no relevance in their daily struggle for survival. As the black Yorkshire footballer and comedian Charlie Williams remarked about his time as a miner in the 1940s: 'My colour didn't matter a bit down the pit. We had no time for daft things like that, and we were all the same colour anyway – coal black.' Alfred Lawes, the son of a West Indian seaman who arrived in South Wales in 1912, remembered how his father and his workmates were accepted into a mining community in Maerdy, about 30 miles from Brynmawr: 'Believe it or not, each one of them – there was four, five I think – uh, were taken home, no questions asked, to be lodgers and to work down the pits with them in Maerdy. ... They were judged not on their colour, but the fact they were men and were willing to work down the pit.'

In September 1906 Lionel married Rebecca Thomas, the daughter of a mixed-race family who had lived in Brynmawr since the early 1880s. Her mother Ruth was a white woman born to a labouring family in Conock, a small village in Wiltshire. By the time Ruth was 18 she was working as a domestic servant in the house of a well-to-do building surveyor in Central London. We do not know how or when she met her husband, William Thomas, but by the early 1880s they were living together in Brynmawr, a small but growing coal and iron town about 30 miles from Cardiff. At over 1,250 feet above sea level, it looked down on the valleys from the north-eastern edge of the South Wales' coalfields. Reputedly the highest town in Wales, it was known affectionately to its inhabitants as the 'City on the Hills'.

William Thomas, Rebecca's father, had to travel somewhat further to get to Brynmawr. A black man descended from a family who lived on the west coast of Africa, he was born to a single mother on St Helena, the tiny island in the middle of the South Atlantic. Like Lionel Francis, William Thomas was a citizen of what historians now call the 'Black Atlantic', in which the Atlantic Ocean was not a barrier but a highway across which men and women travelled back and forth from Africa, Britain, the West Indies and America. The Atlantic was a route to find work, a connection for families, and a network which ensured that the trials and tribulations, not to mention the triumphs, of its black communities were well-known.

St Helena was so isolated from the rest of the world that Britain exiled Napoleon there after his defeat at Waterloo in 1815, safe in the knowledge that escape was all but impossible. The British colonists on the island used enslaved people to work for them, but after Britain abolished slavery in 1838, St Helena became a temporary home for Africans who had been removed from slave ships by the Royal Navy. One of those enslaved people was Mary Thomas, whose daughter, also named Mary, gave birth to a son, William Thomas, in April 1860. We do not know how William made his way from St Helena to Wales or how he met Ruth but by 1883 he was working as a labourer in Brynmawr. In June that year William and Ruth had a daughter, Rebecca. Seven more children, five boys and two girls, would follow, with the last being born in 1904.

Life was hard for working people in Wales in the 1900s, but it was even tougher for black families like the Francises. Three months after Rebecca and Lionel got married in 1906, and just two weeks before Christmas, they were evicted from the two rooms they were renting in Brynmawr's Alexandra Place. An altercation ensued and Lionel was arrested and charged with assault. Despite Rebecca testifying that Lionel had not assaulted anyone, he was found guilty and fined five shillings. A week later, Heber Huggins, the landlord who had evicted them, got into the same train carriage as Lionel on his way to work. Angry that Huggins would 'not stop saying things about him', Lionel offered to fight him on the station platform. Huggins refused and reported him to the police. When the case came to court, Lionel was found guilty of threatening behaviour, and fined £5. Lionel objected to the verdict and told the court that 'I am not willing to suffer when I am innocent'. The judge informed him that if he didn't pay he would be sent to jail, so he reluctantly accepted the fine.

Racist assaults on black men were not unknown in the valleys. In 1900 in Nantyglo, just a couple of miles from Brynmawr, Thomas Barnes and George Watkins were convicted of assaulting a local black man, Thomas Smith. Racism was fuelled by newspapers promoting fear of black men's relationships with white women through luridly racist headlines such as the *South Wales Gazette*'s 'Should Black Man Marry White Woman?' [sic] or the *Dundee Evening Post*'s 'Negroes as Colliers Have No Difficulty In Getting White Wives'. Lionel Francis felt acutely the constant gnawing grip of this racism. At the end of January 1905, he found himself singled out by his employer, the Lancaster Steam Coal Company, and sacked from his check-weigher's job simply because 'he was not wanted'. He sued the company for wrongful dismissal and was awarded one month's wages by the judge. What role race played in his dismissal is impossible to know, but during the course of the hearing in April 1905, Lionel told the court he had applied for 31 other jobs since January and had been turned down for all of them, saying that 'amongst other reasons given being objections to the plaintiff's race'.

By 1911 he was no longer a check-weigher but working at the coal face as a hewer, digging the coal out of the ground with a shovel and a pickaxe. Even so, he continued preaching in the chapels around Brynmawr. In September 1909 he conducted three services in one day for 'large congregations' who gathered to celebrate the anniversary of the Zion Baptist Christian Endeavourer's chapel in Abertillery. He and Rebecca now had a daughter, Olive, born in March 1907, and for a few years the marriage appeared to be going smoothly. However, Lionel's preaching seems to have come to an end at some point before World War One broke out in August 1914. Despite the relative security of jobs in the mining industry during the war, it appears that Lionel's loss of status within the community had an adverse effect on his mental health.

His marriage to Rebecca began to collapse as he became violent towards her. They separated in September 1916 after he had beaten and held her by the throat. A reconciliation took place in March 1917 but by the autumn of 1918 Lionel was complaining that 'married life had not been very pleasant' and had put Rebecca's belongings out on the street. Family tensions boiled over in September 1918 when Rebecca's brother Joe visited Lionel to confront him about what Lionel told the subsequent court hearing was a 'slanderous' issue. Whether this was about the impending birth of the baby who would become Roy Francis to the teenaged Alice May Evans isn't clear, but it resulted in the two men, aided by Joe's wife Rosa, brawling in the street. Frustrated by a society that judged him by his colour, Lionel's life was descending into chaos, poisoning all those around him.

BLACK COMMUNITIES UNDER SIEGE

In the summer of 1919, the lives of black Welsh people in Cardiff, Newport and Barry descended into hell, the memory of which would become seared into the minds of the Francis family and black communities around Britain. On Wednesday 11 June, 1919, racist riots broke out in Cardiff's Tiger Bay, less than a mile from where Roy was born earlier that year. It began when a gang of white men attacked a bus bringing home a group of black men and white women from a day out. To defend themselves, some of the black men fired revolver shots – guns being commonplace in the years after World War One. The growing mob forced its way into Tiger Bay, setting fire to and ransacking houses belonging to black families. Over the next four days, groups of white vigilantes rampaged through Cardiff's docklands, attacking black men, houses, and businesses. When the dust settled, three men were dead, and 28 people appeared in court charged with a variety of offences. The non-white defendants all received harsher sentences than their white attackers.

Cardiff was not the only place where black communities were attacked. The week before the Tiger Bay events, a racist mob ran riot in Newport, attacking the homes of black people, a Chinese laundry and a Greek boarding house. Among the rioters arrested were star rugby union three-quarter Jerry Shea and his teammate, William Haley. Shea was accused of axing down the door of the home of John Davies, a black man married to a white woman, and trying to set the house alight. He was found not guilty of riotous assembly but bound over for 12 months, while Haley was convicted and also bound over for a year. The following January, Shea was picked for Wales against England, when he became the first player to score a try, conversion, penalty and drop goal in the same international match. In December 1921 he switched codes and signed for Wigan rugby league club.

Another future Wigan player also experienced the impact of the riots in Newport. Ten-year-old George Bennett lived with his Jamaican father and white Welsh mother up the road in Pontymister, and they were equally fearful of becoming victims of the mob. A decade later Bennett would leave Wales for Wigan and become the first black international rugby league player. The second was Alec Givvons, who was then living with his mixed-race family in the centre of Newport. They escaped the attacks but Givvons' father was later detained by police twice in the same week for not having the correct papers, despite the fact that as a British subject he did not need them, and he was forced to register as an alien. Such events were not easily forgotten by those who experienced them.

As well as in Cardiff and Newport, 1919 also saw racist mobs attack black, Arab and Chinese communities in the dockland areas of Barry, Glasgow, London, Salford, South Shields, and Liverpool. Almost all these riots began with objections to white women's relationships with black men, but the underlying cause was the collapse of merchant shipping at the end of the war, when shipowners immediately sacked thousands of seamen of all races. When it came to jobs, black, Arab and Chinese sailors found themselves overlooked. 'Every morning we go down to shipping offices to find ourselves work as to make an honest bread and are bluntly refused on account of our colour,' complained one black seaman in Cardiff. For discharged white Royal and Merchant Navy sailors desperately seeking work, the long-established Arab, African, Chinese and West Indian sea-faring communities in Britain became the scapegoat.

The 1919 riots had a profound and long-lasting impact on black communities. A quarter of a century later, the sociologist Kenneth Little discovered that they had 'left a considerable mark on the social heritage of the coloured community, and even to-day its older members base their uncompromising attitude towards white people largely on various incidents, real as well as alleged, which then took place in Cardiff'. In 1950 a *Picture Post* story about Tiger Bay described the community's 'vivid recollection of race riots'. These shocking events led many black people to search for new political answers. Some looked towards Marcus Garvey's Universal Negro Improvement Association (UNIA) and its programme of black pride, separatism and 'Africa for the Africans, at home and abroad'. Born in Jamaica in 1887, Marcus Garvey formed the UNIA in 1914. In 1917 he set up its first American branch and by the summer of 1920 he claimed a global membership of two million people across the USA, Central America, West Africa and the West Indies. In Britain, UNIA branches were set up in London, Cardiff and Barry. Among the many people attracted to Marcus Garvey's message was Lionel Francis.

But as Lionel's interest in politics grew, his relationship with Rebecca became increasingly violent and dysfunctional. In the spring of 1920, Lionel's behaviour towards Rebecca had become so bad that their 12-year-old daughter Olive left the family home to stay with her grandmother, Ruth. She later told Brynmawr Police Court that Lionel had beaten her mother three or four times in her presence. In April, Rebecca decided she had had enough and applied for a legal separation because of Lionel's persistent cruelty. Shockingly, after hearing how Lionel had hit Rebecca with a basin during an argument about how his meals were cooked, the magistrate dismissed Rebecca's case on the grounds that her claim of persistent cruelty had not been proved.

Even so, the marriage was clearly at an end, and in July 1920 Lionel booked a passage to New York on the ocean-going liner the SS *Imperator* and set sail to begin a new life in America. He would never set foot in Wales again.

In a different way, Rebecca also began a new life. She had adopted – informally, as there was no legal system of adoption in Britain until 1926 – her husband's baby son, Roy. For a wife to adopt the child of her husband's extra-marital relationship may seem unusual, but Rebecca, as remembered by her two grandsons, was an extremely warm and loving person. Moreover, her experience of life would have shown how difficult and traumatic growing up in an orphanage could be for a black child, so from the moment the infant Roy came into her home, he was treated as nothing less than her own son. She even added Lionel's name to his, making him Roy Lionel Francis. Rebecca's spirit of generosity would be the basis for everything the baby boy would achieve in his life.

BRYNMAWR BOY

Roy's adoption by Rebecca gave him a stable and loving home, but growing up in Brynmawr during the 1920s and 1930s was hard. Rebecca never remarried and she, Roy, and his half-sister Olive lived in just two rooms of a house in King Street, near the centre of the town. A short walk away, Rebecca's five brothers, two sisters and their families lived next door to each other in the same two rows of terraced housing on Windsor Road. A month after Roy's fourth birthday, his adoptive cousin Megan – the daughter of Rebecca's sister Dorcas – died of bronchitis, a common illness made deadly by poverty.

Four of Roy's uncles worked underground at local collieries when jobs were available, while a fifth found work repairing coal-wagons in nearby Blaina. Rebecca herself worked as a domestic servant, and her sister Dorcas was an elementary school teacher. Nor were they the only black people in the town. A 1927 photograph of Brynmawr rugby club's players and officials shows an unidentified black man as part of the group. In July 1929 Olive married Francis Sinclair, a black seaman who also lived near the centre of Brynmawr. Together, the extended Francis and Thomas families created a small black community in the town which exists still today.

As Roy grew up, unemployment was sweeping through the Welsh valleys. The region's coal industry virtually collapsed and in 1930 the unemployment rate in South Wales topped 27 per cent. Over 400,000 people abandoned hope in the 1920s and 1930s and left Wales in search of jobs elsewhere. Things in Brynmawr were even worse. 'Nowhere in the coalfield,' wrote Hilda Jennings in her 1934 book, *Brynmawr. A Study of a Distressed Area*, 'has unemployment been more prolonged, or the accompanying economic, social and spiritual distress been so acute.' By the early 1930s half of the town's working population were unemployed.

For boys of Roy's generation the outlook was bleak. More than a third of the town's youths who left school between 1926 and 1929 could not find work, and another 20 per cent had to leave Brynmawr to get a job. Such grinding daily poverty was too much for some. When a local demonstration against unemployment was banned by the local authorities in March 1935, *The Times* reported that it was broken up when 'police with batons charged the crowd, and hundreds of unemployed men took up positions on a slag tip overlooking the road and pelted the police with stones'.

Roy also faced an additional obstacle. The colour of his skin made things much more difficult for him. A so-called 'colour bar' operated in many parts of Britain, excluding black and non-white people from certain jobs, housing areas, pubs and hotels, and even competing at the highest levels of some sports. When he was writing his pioneering study of black people in South Wales in the 1940s, Kenneth Little was told by one black interviewee that: 'At present no coloured boy or girl can procure a job in an office no matter how qualified he or she may be. Indeed, as a matter of fact, they cannot secure a job in any capacity whatsoever. No engineering works will employ them and apart from shipping they have no other outlet.' In 1934, the League of Coloured Peoples, one of the earliest British anti-racist organisations, surveyed Cardiff and estimated that 80 per cent of black men were unemployed and that 'their home life was reduced to a bare subsistence level'.

They were also subject to harassment from the police. Shortly before Roy's half-sister Olive got married in 1929, Albert Thomas, her uncle and brother of Rebecca, was convicted of using obscene language against a policeman in the town's Market Square. This was a common way of dealing with working-class people who challenged police intimidation, and Albert flatly denied he had been swearing. Despite the magistrate finding no evidence against him, Albert was ordered to pay the costs of the case.

Living with racism, poverty and stress almost inevitably warped and strained relationships. Olive began to suffer the same problems with her husband as Rebecca had with Lionel. Eighteen months after he married Olive, Francis Sinclair was charged with assaulting her. The court heard that Francis had been violent towards her even on their wedding day, and on one occasion had held a knife to her throat. Despite Rebecca and her sister-in-law Gladys Thomas describing the 'perfect dread' under which Olive lived, the court refused to grant her a legal separation from her husband. Condemned to live with her husband's violence, Olive increasingly suffered health problems. In May 1933, while suffering from an attack of acute gastroenteritis, she died of a heart attack aged just 26.

As he grew up and became more aware of the world around him, Roy would have had to come to terms with the psychological burden of racism. Rebecca would have grappled with the moment when, in the words of James Baldwin, she was confronted with how to 'prepare the child for the day when the child would

be despised and how to create in the child – by what means –
a stronger antidote to this poison than one had found for one's
self'. Mixed-race children like Roy were routinely accused of being
genetically incapable of forming stable relationships or working in
anything but the most menial jobs. Notoriously, the birth-control
campaigner Marie Stopes called for mixed-race children to be
sterilised, arguing that, 'The unhappy fate of he who is neither black
nor white is prevented from being passed on to yet more unborn
babes.' A 1930 report titled 'Investigation into the Colour Problem
in Liverpool and Other Ports' insultingly used the derogatory term
'half-caste' – which implied mixed-race people were less than whole
and lacked any status – and claimed that 'half-caste children on
the whole appear to be below the average', that they were leading
'very disharmonious lives', and 'tend[ed] to give undue prominence
to sex; owing to the nature of the houses in which they live their
moral standards are extraordinarily low'.

Just as the 1919 riots left deep physical and mental scars on
the black community, this daily stigmatising of black and mixed-
race people created what one of Kenneth Little's interviewees
described as 'a colour bar from within'. This, he argued, caused
a black person to 'instinctively hold back from certain things.
He is afraid of being humiliated. He is so terribly sensitive,
and always anxious to preserve his self-respect'. Fifty years
after the publication of the Liverpool report, sociologist Mark
Christian found that some of the older members of the city's
black community still resented the report and the unwelcome
publicity it brought. Although Roy would rarely discuss it, his
early experiences of being a black child in a white world would
shape the rest of his life, becoming both the secret of his success
and also the curse which forever haunted him.

LIONEL FRANCIS REINVENTS HIMSELF

The same was also true of Roy's father Lionel, whose desire to
outrun and escape racism had led him to America. On 8 August,
1920, Lionel disembarked the SS *Imperator* in New York and made

his way to Harlem. Since the start of the 20th century, Harlem had become home for hundreds of thousands of African Americans and substantial numbers of Caribbean migrants, boosting New York's black population five-fold to 328,000 in 1930. Coming from the tiny and isolated black community in Brynmawr to the seething, intense, and endlessly stimulating 'city within a city' of Harlem must have been a liberating experience for Lionel. The Jamaican poet and revolutionary Claude McKay had made a similar journey a few years earlier and recalled it was 'like entering into a paradise of my own people when at last I fell into the dark warm throbbing bosom of Harlem'. At last, Lionel was in a place where he could develop his talents to the full.

Shortly after he arrived, he went to New York's Madison Square Garden to be a delegate at the first international convention of the Universal Negro Improvement Association (UNIA). He was one of a reported 20,000 people who endorsed the convention's *Declaration of the Rights of the Negro Peoples of the World* calling for the unity and self-reliance of black people around the world, and backing emigration to Africa. News of the huge gathering travelled quickly around the world, and even British Intelligence took an interest, reporting to the government that, 'At a recent convention in New York at which Marcus Garvey presided 15,000 American citizens of African descent "pledged their sacred blood to free Africa".' This led to the UNIA newspaper, the *Negro World*, being banned in several British colonies in the Caribbean.

How Lionel became a delegate to the convention has proved impossible to trace. His name does not appear in any accounts of the UNIA in Britain, and its British branches did not send delegates to the international convention. Regardless of how he came to attend it, the convention changed Lionel's life. He moved to Philadelphia and quickly rose to become president of the city's UNIA branch. He also invented a new life story for himself. He became Dr Lionel Francis, a physician who had studied at Howard University (the historically black university in Washington DC), qualified at Edinburgh University School of Medicine, and practised in London.

None of this was remotely true. Yet it undoubtedly reflected Lionel's belief in what he could have achieved if his life had not been constrained by the straitjacket of racism for his first 40 years. If a poor black migrant to South Wales could become a respected member of an overwhelmingly white community and a well-regarded local preacher, how much more could he have achieved in a favourable environment? He was not the only person in the transatlantic black community trying to rebalance his life chances. There was a thriving underground market for fake medical degrees and other qualifications on board the ships which took migrants to and fro across the Atlantic. A certificate from the 'East African School of Medicine and Surgery' could be purchased for $2.75 on board at least one tramp steamer. This was an era in which electrical communications and media were in their infancy, so the chance that anyone would notice such deceptions was small. And as a man of great charm and charisma, who would suspect that Dr Lionel Francis was not who he claimed to be?

His *bona fides* were questioned only once. In April 1922 he was taken to court for practising medicine without a licence by the Pennsylvania State Board of Health, who demanded he be deported. Lionel was one of 50 people indicted by the Board's investigator Dr Louis Saltzman, who was waging a campaign against 'quack doctors'. It was a campaign aimed at Philadelphia's black community, and rounded up not only obvious fraudsters but also doctors who had studied at medical schools in countries whose qualifications were considered to 'have no standing' in America. Despite a large number of protesters attending his bail hearing, the evidence suggested that Lionel's American adventure was about to come to an abrupt end.

But then fate intervened. Two months after Lionel's indictment, Saltzman himself was arrested on charges of extortion. He had demanded $300 from the Philadelphia County Chiropractors' Association in exchange for providing its members with medical practitioner certificates. Eventually the chiropractors called the police, who recorded Saltzman demanding kickbacks of $200 a month and a car in return for his services. He was found guilty, sentenced to three months in jail and fined $100. Its evidence now terminally tainted, the prosecution against Lionel was quietly dropped.

Freed from the threat of deportation, Lionel's political career now soared even higher. As well as being a key figure in Philadelphia, he also became a national leader of the UNIA and worked closely with Marcus Garvey himself. But then a bombshell dropped. On 30 August, 1924, the *New York Age*, one of America's leading black weeklies, carried the sensational headline 'Garvey is Dishonest. Dr Lionel Francis Tells Why He Quit as President of the Philadelphia UNIA'. Spread over three pages, Lionel explained that he and other Philadelphia UNIA members had loaned Garvey thousands of dollars which he refused to repay. He accused Garvey of 'bad management, lies, attempts at dishonesty, crime and immorality'. Lionel resigned from the UNIA on 1 June and quickly set up his own organisation, the International Alliance of Negroes (IAN), with branches in Philadelphia and New York.

Lionel's IAN essentially continued the work of the Philadelphia UNIA. In August 1925 it announced it was opening a new headquarters on Lombard Street in central Philadelphia, which also offered medical and dental facilities. In a major speech early in 1926 Lionel – titled the 'Supreme President' of the IAN – argued that black people had been let down by the existing political parties and had to organise 'a political organisation of a different character'. It would not be long, he explained, 'until the Negro would have a new sense of political consciousness, unite all his voting forces and thus secure needed reforms for the race as a whole.'

By this time Lionel's personal life had also changed. When he left England in 1920, he had named Rebecca Francis as his next of kin on his departure documents. But on 6 January, 1927 he married Maizie King, the former secretary of the Philadelphia UNIA. Six months later, on 17 July, she gave birth to a baby boy, who the couple named Lionel Almeido Francis. There is no evidence that Lionel and Rebecca were ever divorced, so we can only assume that Lionel had decided that his old life was now definitely over, with no prospect of him ever returning to Wales nor of his family joining him in America. Apart from claiming to have been educated at Oxford and Edinburgh, Lionel would never publicly refer to his life in Britain again.

Nor would he ever know of the achievements of the boy he abandoned in Brynmawr. Yet the same qualities that had made Lionel a prominent public figure – intelligence, charisma, and an instinctive sense of leadership – would soon begin to manifest themselves in his son.

A BRYNMAWR 'INVINCIBLE'

Roy was baptised in Brynmawr's Anglican church in March 1923, and in December 1923 he was enrolled in the infants section of Brynmawr Council School. Most children started school during the year they turned four but Rebecca gave his date of birth as 20 November, 1918, which meant he could start school before his actual fourth birthday. We don't know if this was a mistake by the school or if Rebecca had deliberately raised his age to get him into school earlier. Given the fact Rebecca had been deserted by her husband it is probable she had to support herself and her two children by working full-time. Getting Roy into school early would have solved the problem of who would look after him while she worked.

As he grew older, Roy became aware of the success of Arthur Dibbin, his father's other son, who had developed a fine baritone singing voice and became a talented trumpet player. In the 1930s Arthur worked with a number of jazz bands, most famously Ken 'Snakehips' Johnson's 'Jamaican Emperors of Jazz'. Arthur was playing with the band at the Café Royale in London in 1941 when it suffered a direct hit from a German bomb, killing Snakehips and 33 other people. Arthur survived and his career continued into the 1950s. Roy would always refer to Arthur as his half-brother – one of the few details of his early life he passed on to his children – and Arthur's success in the 1930s would also have given the teenage Roy a glimpse of the possibilities that lay beyond Brynmawr.

Perhaps inspired by Arthur, the teenage Roy was clearly ambitious and determined to improve his lot in life. He was a chorister at the local Anglican church, where the vicar described him as 'honest, industrious and cheerful', and spent two years working as a volunteer office boy for the Brynmawr Community Study Council. The study council had been set up as part of a Quaker project to relieve poverty in the coalfields, which also led to a furniture factory being opened in the town and an outdoor swimming pool built by local volunteers. 'Honest, very active and willing, and keen to get on,' was the verdict passed by the manager of the Study Council on young Roy.

By the time he received these glowing references, Roy was a pupil at Brynmawr Council School for Boys. It prided itself on its rugby prowess, and the school team had been dubbed the 'Brynmawr Invincibles' by the local press. Like many other headmasters in Welsh schools, Brynmawr's Mr William Morris-Jones was a keen fan of the game and believed in its educational importance for his boys. Coached by rugby master Dickie Neat, a well-known local personality in the game, the team was unbeaten for seven seasons from 1930. Roy could have had no better nursery in which to learn and develop rugby skills, and he soon became 'a rugby football player of the first order', according to his woodwork teacher, Mr Morgan. By the time he left school in 1934, Roy was captain of the Invincibles.

Rugby wasn't the first sport he took an active interest in. There was also a family connection to boxing. Roy told journalists in the late 1950s that he had trained as a boy with an uncle who was a trainer to Gipsy Daniels, the Llanelli-born light-heavyweight who won the British championship in 1927. He would retain his interest in the fight game throughout his life. His teenage athletic talents were also directed towards water sports. In July 1932 the new outdoor swimming pool was opened just 10 minutes' walk from the Francis home. We can assume Roy spent considerable time at the lido, not least because in August 1933 he won a diving contest held there. Later that month, on August Bank Holiday weekend, he excelled on the dry land of the athletics track. Still just 14 years old, Roy finished third in a 120 yards sprint contest open to sprinters under 16 at the local British Legion sports' day.

The sports' day was held at the ground of Brynmawr Rugby Club, one of the smaller cogs in the mighty machinery of Welsh rugby union. Almost totally eclipsed by nearby powerhouse teams like Ebbw Vale and Abertillery, it had only ever produced one Welsh international player, William Evans, who signed for Leeds rugby league club shortly after winning his Wales cap in 1911. Even so, the importance of the sport meant the rugby club was the premier sporting institution in Brynmawr. In 1934 it had around 60 members, more than the local cricket club and twice as many as the town's soccer club. Roy later explained how he turned up to watch a pre-season training match at the club but one of the teams was a player short and he was asked to play. He made such an impression in the match that he was selected to play for Brynmawr in its first game of the 1936–37 season at Risca.

He was now beginning to mature into a young man. He stood five feet 10 inches tall, weighed 12 stone four pounds, and was good-looking, making him the most distinctive of the new players who took to the field for Brynmawr's opening match. Although the inexperienced team lost by six points, the rugby reporter for the *Merthyr Express* noted that 'Roy Francis, the left-wing, showed much promise'. This would prove to be something of an understatement. The following week Brynmawr played their first home match of the season against Newport's mighty Pill Harriers, who had provided many players to the Welsh national side and won the Monmouthshire League numerous times. In a major upset, the young Brynmawr team defeated them 12-3. Roy scored one of his side's two tries, and the *Express* once again singled him out by predicting he had 'a great future'. The team lost its next match 9-3 away at Blackwood but returned to winning ways at home the following week, coming back from a 7-0 half-time deficit to win 9-7 against a strong Merthyr team. Once again Roy earned praise for scoring a 'smart try'.

This was the last game he played for Brynmawr. Indeed, except for wartime, it would be the last game of rugby union he ever played. After the game against Merthyr, Roy was approached by a scout from Wigan and asked if he would like to play in a trial game with a view to signing for one of the most famous clubs in rugby league. The scout was Arthur Fairfax, who had been a talent-spotter for various league clubs since the mid-1920s. In 1954, Fairfax was the man who unsuccessfully tried to persuade Carwyn James, the Llanelli fly-half and future coach of the British Lions, to play rugby league for Oldham. At the same time as he was speaking to Roy, Fairfax also approached Newport forward Trevor Foster about signing for Wigan, and suggested that Trevor could travel up to Wigan with Roy. However, Foster told him he felt he had a chance of being selected for Wales the next season and turned down his offer. But he didn't win a cap, and he signed for Bradford the following season.

Roy had no such hopes of being selected to play for Wales' national team. No black player had ever worn Wales' scarlet jersey, and none would do so until the 1980s. It was widely understood that no rugby union player of colour would be picked for Wales. But in rugby league, George Bennett and Alec Givvons, the two black Welsh players from Newport who had experienced the 1919 riots at first-hand, were already starring for Wales. Because he was not yet 21, Roy needed the permission of his mother Rebecca to sign for Wigan. Regardless of the money her son would be paid to play rugby league, Rebecca would have to be sure that he would not face the dangers and humiliations of racial prejudice when he was so far away from home. She needed to be convinced that he was moving to a better life.

After much thought, she gave her blessing to the move, and Roy set off on the long train journey north to the heart of the Lancashire coalfields. Keeping his identity a secret by playing for Wigan's 'A' (reserve) team as A. N. Other – if the RFU discovered a union player playing rugby league, he would be banned for life – Roy impressed the Wigan management sufficiently that after featuring in a 14-6 win over Warrington's 'A' team on 14 November, 1936 he was offered a professional contract with a £400 signing-on fee. He accepted immediately, and three days later the local Wigan newspapers announced that 'Lionel Roy Francis, centre three-quarter' had signed for the club.

Aged just 17 years and nine months, Roy Francis was a professional rugby league player. His life, and eventually the sport of rugby league, would never be the same.

2

On The Road to and from Wigan Pier: 1936–1939

'Racialism is like pain. It's a very, very personal thing.'

To make the 170-mile train journey from Brynmawr to Wigan and begin a new life would have been daunting for any 17-year-old, but Roy was following a well-trodden path and would have immediately felt at home in Wigan. Coal and rugby were the most obvious similarities between South Wales and West Lancashire, but Wigan's friendly working-class community and proximity to the countryside would also have reminded him of Brynmawr.

He was the latest in a long line of Welsh rugby players who had 'Gone North' to capitalise on their rugby talents. Ever since 1884, when Llanelli's international full-back Harry Bowen signed for Dewsbury, hundreds had travelled to all points in the rugby league heartlands, and Wigan had had more than its fair share. In December 1904 the club signed the centre three-quarter Bert Jenkins and scrum-half Johnny Thomas, the first of its many Welsh players who went on to play international rugby league. The greatest of them all was Jim Sullivan, the prodigious Cardiff full-back who signed for the club for the huge sum of £750 in 1921. Like Roy, he was just 17 when he took the road to Wigan Pier, beginning a career which would see him acclaimed as one of the giants of rugby league.

By the time that Roy arrived in Wigan, the Welsh connection ran through the club's history like blue scars on a miner's hands. Sullivan held the team records for most goals and appearances, while Port Talbot-born Johnny Ring held the record for most tries, scored at the unbelievable rate of more than one every match. Indeed, Wigan's cosmopolitan recruitment policy was one of the hallmarks of its success, as chairman Harry Lowe pointed out in 1926. 'We have seven Welshmen, three South Africans, one Cumbrian, one player from the Manchester district and only one local,' he told the press, while admitting that without their imported players, 'Wigan would become a second- or third-rate side'.

As Roy quickly discovered, nothing other than being a first-rate side was acceptable to the club, its supporters, or the town itself. Ever since the first Wigan rugby club had been formed in 1872, the sport had been a prominent symbol of local civic pride. In 1894, as rugby's dispute over 'broken-time' payments was coming to a head, Wigan was one of three Lancashire clubs suspended by the Rugby Football Union for allegedly paying their players in contravention of the game's strict amateur laws. The following year they were one of the 22 founding members of the breakaway Northern Union, which would later become known as rugby league. After moving into the purpose-built Central Park amphitheatre in 1902, Wigan became one of the game's major powers.

The team's success became even more important during the hard, hungry years between the wars. Like many towns in northern England, Wigan had the Industrial Revolution to thank for its prominence. Originally the site of a Roman settlement, it was an unremarkable town until it became a stronghold of support for Charles I during the English Civil War of the 1640s. Over the next century it was involved in the Jacobite risings and welcomed Bonnie Prince Charlie. The town's motto, which would also be adopted by its rugby league club, was 'Ancient and Loyal', reflecting its fealty to the Royalist cause. But it was the coming of industry at the end of the 1700s which put Wigan on the map. Textile mills sprang up across its horizon and by the early years of the Victorian era it was a centre of the cotton industry. Its rich coal deposits led to dozens of mine shafts being sunk across the area. Its famous pier was built on the Leeds to Liverpool Canal to load coal from local pits onto barges for countless onward destinations. By the start of the 20th century, it was a town of over 80,000 people at the heart of the industrial north of England.

Like Brynmawr, its strength became its weakness during the inter-war years. The collapse of the cotton and coal markets sent the town spinning into decline. In 1930, 15,000 people in the town were unemployed, and 60 per cent of its cotton mills and 17 of its 40 pits shut down in the 1930s. The town's reputation as a byword for deprivation was capitalised on by George Orwell in his 1937 book, *The Road to Wigan Pier*. The Old Etonian painted a miserable picture of the town and its people. He believed that working-class people he met there did not 'show much capacity for leadership' and that the working man 'does not act, [but] he is acted upon'. Yet in reality Wigan had a thriving cultural and political life. As the illustrated weekly *Picture Post* reported in 1939, the town was host to the seventh-largest public library in Britain, had a thriving adult education scene – 'Wiganers are passionately keen on education' noted the *Post* – and many places of popular entertainment. Among the many aspects of that cultural life that Orwell did not notice – but the *Picture Post* did – was Wigan rugby league club.

Unlike Brynmawr, Wigan did not have even a small black community. The only written record of a black presence in the town is the memoir of Olive Harleston, a black woman who was born in Wigan in 1906. She lived in the centre of the town until the 1920s, when she went to live in America. Looking back from the 1980s, she remembered herself as the only black person in Wigan at that time. Olive's parents were black Americans working in the town who, for reasons that were never explained to her, fostered their child to a midwife in Wigan when they returned to America. She could recall no sense of being different to her school friends and remembered only one instance of racist name-calling when she was at school, for which the boy was told off by the teacher. She lamented that it was only when she went to live with her parents in Philadelphia that she experienced overt racial discrimination. Olive had no interest in sport but, perhaps demonstrating that you could take the girl out of Wigan but not Wigan out of the girl, the one thing she always missed about living in the town was its famous pies.

By the time Roy arrived in Wigan in November 1936, there was probably only one other black Briton living in Wigan: George Bennett, the outstanding former Newport player, who had signed for Wigan in August 1931. In 1934 he wore the number six shirt when Wigan defeated Salford to lift the Championship Trophy and also topped the club's try-scoring chart that season. The following year he made his international debut for Wales against France – making him the first-ever black rugby league international – and he went on to play two more internationals, coming into contention for the 1936 Great Britain tour of Australia and New Zealand. In December 1937, George transferred to Bradford, where he played until the end of World War Two.

Bennett was not the only person of colour in the Wigan ranks during the early 1930s. In 1927 the club signed Māori forward Len Mason, a dominant force in the New Zealand team that toured Britain in 1926. Strong in the scrum and smart with the ball in hand – he could play as a centre three-quarter when needed – he became a lynchpin of Wigan's forward pack for nine seasons. As Mason and Bennett showed, Wigan's quest to recruit the best players wherever they could find them seems not to have been hindered by racial prejudice, and highlighted that when it came to racial integration, rugby league was somewhat different from the rest of British sport.

SPORT AND RACE IN THE INTERWAR YEARS

When the young Roy opened the sports pages of newspapers in the 1930s, it is unlikely he would have seen anyone who looked like him. Indeed, British sport in the interwar years was almost completely white. Of the 4000 or so professional soccer players who turned out for Football League clubs between the wars, there seems to have been only three players of African descent. No black players appear to have played for any of the Scottish Football League's clubs during this time. Of the three playing in England, Welshman Eddie Parris turned out once for Wales in 1931, Plymouth Argyle's Jack Leslie was seemingly named in a 1925 England squad and then mysteriously removed amid suspicions of racism, and Alf Charles made a single appearance for Southampton in 1937. There were of course black footballers playing outside of the Football League – for example, Jimmie Clarke played for Everton reserves but was never selected for the first team, and *The Keys*, published by the League of Coloured Peoples, pointed to a black teenager who was captain of his school football team in 1937 – but records remain frustratingly sparse.

Things were even worse in cricket. No black cricketers played county cricket during the interwar years. 'The thought of a black man taking the place of a white man in our side was anathema. It was as simple as that,' recalled Lancashire and England all-rounder Len Hopwood. A very small number of West Indian players did turn out as professionals in local league cricket in the Midlands and north of England. Most famous was the West Indian test cricketer Learie Constantine, who starred for Nelson in the Lancashire League from 1928 to 1937. His fellow Trinidadian, the Southampton footballer Alf Charles, also played for Nelson in 1935 and 1936, while the fast bowler Alf Francis, who had starred on the 1923 West Indies' tour of England, played for Seaham Harbour in the Durham League in 1929. A few black British cricketers played at lower levels of the game, such as a fast bowler named Thompson who played for Bentley Colliery in 1922 and H. Holinsinge who played for Thorncliffe in the Yorkshire Council Cricket League in 1930, but the historical record has yet to be thoroughly investigated.

In Roy's original code of rugby union, no black player was selected for any of the Four 'Home Nations' teams during the interwar years. Plymouth's Jimmy Peters, who played four times for England between 1906 and 1908, was the single exception to the uniformly white British and Irish national teams which played between the first international rugby match in 1872 and Mark Brown's selection for Wales in 1983. There were black players at lower levels of the sport, notably in Wales, but the snow-blindingly white tone of the game's elite strongly suggests that an informal colour bar existed in the sport. This certainly appears to be true in Wales, where black players of remarkable talent were always passed over by national selectors. The only black Welsh rugby players of that era who are remembered today are those who went north to play rugby league; to continue to play in Wales meant a career of unfulfilled obscurity for black players. This lack of black representation in the Welsh national team was a glaring contradiction to anyone familiar with daily life in Cardiff and its vibrant black and mixed-race community. Ros Sullivan, the white wife of Cardiff-born Clive Sullivan – who captained the Great Britain team that won the Rugby League World Cup in 1972 – recalled visiting her husband's Welsh relatives in the 1960s: 'You never saw a black person in the Welsh rugby union side. But until I went down to Wales, I'd never seen so many mixed-race couples.'

Athletics was little different. Despite Harry Edward, a black British teacher who had been raised in Germany, winning bronze medals in the 100m and 200m at the 1920 Olympics in Antwerp, other black athletes found it almost impossible to rise to the top. Like rugby union, golf and tennis at that time, athletics was based on a club structure, in which social activities were often as important as sporting endeavour. This meant that exclusion, whether on the basis of race or class, was rife. This was also true in university athletics. In the summer of 1937 the Black British magazine *The Keys* reported on a recent survey which 'revealed that a freezing out in athletics was going on against the coloured students'. The fact that black student athletes were young middle-class men training to be solicitors, doctors or politicians made little difference. Learie Constantine fought a famous legal case in 1943 against the Imperial Hotel in London's Russell Square over its racist treatment of him. In London to play cricket for the British Dominions' representative team, he was thrown out of the hotel purely because of the colour of skin. A few years earlier he had reserved a hotel room in Brighton but was turned away when the receptionist saw him. Such racist hotel practices were also a threat to sports tournaments. The 1938 World Table Tennis Championships were almost cancelled when it proved virtually impossible to book hotel rooms for the non-white players in London.

As Roy would have been aware from his youthful involvement in the ring, the one sport with a long record of black participation was boxing. As far back as the early 1800s black boxers had been prominent in the sport, and by the start of the 20th century, they were well-established at all levels. In March 1907, the black South African boxer Andrew Jeptha won the British welterweight title, but political anxieties about the British Empire's future meant that Jeptha's short-lived title (he lost it to Joe White five months later) caused outrage. Those fears became rampant in 1911 when the white British heavyweight 'Bombardier' Billy Wells announced he would fight Jack Johnson for the world title in London in October. Politicians and clergymen protested against the fight, believing that the possibility of a white Briton being defeated by a proud and outspoken black man like Johnson was a threat to public order and the Empire's racial hierarchy. On 26 September the Home Office, led by the Home Secretary Winston Churchill, decided the fight was not in 'the best interests of the nation and empire' and banned it. Almost immediately, the British boxing authorities introduced a 'colour bar' which stipulated that British boxing titles could only be contested by British subjects 'born of white parents'. In 1926, the Manchester fighter Len Johnson won the British Empire middleweight championship in Sydney, only to be stripped of the title because he didn't have two white parents. Although the colour bar was opposed by the boxers' union and many other people in Britain, it remained in place until 1948.

Rugby league was the one partial exception to this depressing picture of British sporting racism. Black players had been playing the game since at least the early 1900s. The Pendlebury amateur club which won the Lancashire Junior Cup in 1903 featured a black player, Hunslet signed Lucius Banks, a black American army quarterback in 1912, while former England fly-half Jimmy Peters found himself driven out of rugby union for accepting testimonial payments and joined Barrow in 1913. Ralph Meheux, a mixed-race player, turned out for Hull during World War One. But it was during the 1930s that black players rose above the limits which other sports had set for them, with George Bennett and Alec Givvons playing for Wales, and the brothers Jim and Val Cumberbatch appearing for England. Roy could feel confident that as a league player, he could go as far as his talent would take him, regardless of the colour of skin.

What made rugby league different from other sports? Much of its openness to players of colour was due to its origins as a sport based on a principle of inclusion. Although its revolt against rugby union in 1895 pivoted on the question of allowing 'broken-time' payments to working-class players who lost wages by taking time off work to play the game, rugby's great split of 1895 was underpinned by a belief that players should be judged by merit and not by social class or financial status. When all was said and done, rugby league largely didn't care about the background of its players as long as they had the ability to win matches.

MAKING A LIFE IN WIGAN

On Saturday 21 November, 1936, four days after his signing was announced by the press, Roy made his professional debut in the Wigan 'A' team (as rugby league reserve sides were called) against Rochdale Hornets' 'A' team at Central Park. On the morning of the match the *Wigan Examiner* helpfully printed a photograph of Roy in his Wigan shirt, collar turned up, and looking confidently into the camera. He played at left centre three-quarter and had the immense good fortune to have as his winger Alf Ellaby. Ellaby was one of rugby league's greatest players. He had made his name at St Helens, where he became one of the few players to score tries at the rate of more than one per match, but had been sold to local rivals Wigan to ease financial problems caused by the Great Depression. Three days short of his 34th birthday on the day of the Rochdale match, the tall and lithe Ellaby was a smart player and a cultured man. It is difficult to imagine a better mentor for a teenager making his official rugby league debut.

As expected, Wigan won at a canter. After 12 minutes, Roy supplied the pass to put Ellaby in the clear to score the first try and the veteran winger went on to score three more tries. Perhaps taking the size of the victory for granted, the *Examiner* praised the debutant for his defensive skills: 'Francis brought off two excellent tackles and was responsible for checking the first Rochdale movement of any note.' As a teenager learning the game, Roy would have expected to spend much of his first few seasons playing in the 'A' team, getting a rugby education and developing his body for the demands of the professional men's game.

This was not just about fitness. Just as in many industrial jobs where young workers were subjected to initiation ceremonies and trials of character, young players were only accepted by older rugby league professionals once they had demonstrated their ability to stand up to pressure and physical violence. Jim Sullivan, who was now Wigan's player-coach, was himself a notoriously aggressive player who expected his players to extract a full pound of flesh from their opponents. Alf Ellaby had earlier fallen out with Sullivan over his refusal to intimidate an opposing young winger making his debut, which might explain why Ellaby was playing with Roy in the 'A' team against Rochdale. Fortunately, Roy seems to have avoided a brutal introduction to the sport, and over the course of his next dozen appearances in the 'A' team he scored seven tries.

A sterner test was to come on Good Friday in 1937 when Roy was called up to replace Wigan's very experienced dual-code international centre, Gwyn Davies. As was traditional, the Good Friday match was a derby against Wigan's historic rivals St Helens. Little more than 10 miles apart, the two clubs had vied to be the dominant force in Lancashire rugby since the 1890s. Their rivalry intensified after the General Strike and miners' lockout of 1926, when miners in St Helens accused Wigan miners of going back to work before the dispute ended. They had, it was claimed in St Helens, eaten the bosses' humble pie, and henceforth Wigan were nicknamed the 'Pie-eaters'. Given the popularity of the pies produced in Wigan – as Olive Harlesden remembered – the nickname came to be interpreted as a comment on Wigan's culinary preferences, and was transformed into an affectionate nickname.

The *Wigan Observer* report on the derby said that Roy 'made a good impression. He handled the ball well and gave [left-winger Jack] Morley a service far better than he has had in many games this season'. This confident debut was crowned with a try in Wigan's 16-3 victory. He played again the next day, Easter Saturday, against near neighbours Leigh. Roy scored a hat-trick in a 51-10 barrage. Again the press highlighted Roy, calling him a star: 'He played a tireless game and looked as fresh at the end as he did at the start, and he certainly gained the confidence of the crowd even if the opposition was weak. Despite the heavy going he showed plenty of speed, and was thrustful at all times. In defence he also showed some effective work and Wigan should have little fear of including him in their side against the bigger "shots" of the rugby league.'

He played in three more first-team matches that season, scoring another hat-trick of tries against York. The next season was mainly spent in the 'A' team, and he played just four times in the first team. At this point Wigan had a very strong three-quarter line, all of whom were internationals – including ex-union British Lion Morley and former All Black Eddie Holder – and Roy was viewed as a work in progress for the future.

He quickly settled into life in Wigan. The club found him a job working on a coal delivery lorry, loading sacks of coal onto a truck and then emptying them in the coal bunkers of homes across the town. It also arranged a room for him at a boarding house run by Ernest and Rachel Austin on Upper Dicconson Street, a short walk from the club's Central Park stadium. A few years earlier, George Bennett had also lodged on the same street when he first came to Wigan. The Austins, like countless Wigan families, had suffered during the Great Depression of the 1930s. The son of a miner, Ernest Austin escaped a life down the pit by becoming a sweet salesman and worked his way up to run his own cake and confectionery business. He and his wife, Rachel, who came from nearby Warrington, were married in 1911, and Irene, their only child, was born in 1914. In the 1920s his business was so successful he could afford to send Rene, as she was known to everyone, to a local private school. However, the business had gone bankrupt, forcing Rene to be taken out of private school and the Austins to open up their home as a boarding house for lodgers. At one point, Ernest and the teenage Rene were even going door to door selling loaves to make ends meet.

As a former schoolboy diving champion, Roy had something in common with his new landlord. In his spare time, Ernest Austin was a keen swimmer and water polo player, and had become a well-known figure on the local sports scene as the chairman of Wigan Swimming club and the president of the Northern Water Polo League. It was through his sporting links that Wigan rugby league club approached him for a suitable room for their talented new arrival from South Wales.

The Austins soon made the teenage lodger feel at home. Rene, tall, red-haired and self-confident, was training to be a children's nurse. She took a shine to the new lodger and, despite the fact she was four years older than Roy, the two began courting, as dating was known then. However, in an echo of his father Lionel's escapades as a lodger with the Dibbin family in 1901, Rene became pregnant in April 1938. Three months later, on 23 July, the couple were hastily married at the local Registry Office. In this, they were no different from numerous other couples in the 1930s who had to marry in haste because of unexpected pregnancy. A 1939 survey found that 22.5 per cent of all women who got married that year were already pregnant. There was nothing unusual about the situation the lovers found themselves in, apart from the fact that Rene was white and Roy was black.

In many families such a relationship would have resulted in the young woman being banished. When jazz singer Cleo Laine's white mother married her Jamaican husband in the 1920s she was immediately and forever disowned by her parents. Not all white people felt this way. When Beatrice Whiteman married her British Guyanan husband Lionel Turpin in Leamington Spa just after World War One, her white family had no objections and enthusiastically helped raise her mixed-race children, one of whom would grow up to be World Middleweight boxing champion Randolph Turpin.

But fear of white women's relationships with black men was rampant in the media during the interwar years. In 1919 the British colonial administrator Ralph Williams told *The Times* that 'intimate association between black or coloured men and white women is a thing of horror'. A decade later the *Daily Herald* published what it claimed were 'disturbing revelations regarding relations between coloured men and white women' in Tiger Bay. This led to the Chief Constable of Cardiff demanding the government introduce laws based on South Africa's 1927 Immorality Act, which made interracial sex a criminal offence punishable by five years in jail. The *Daily Telegraph* followed suit with the headline 'Colour Problem in Britain. Menace of Mixed Unions'.

Rene was made of sterner stuff, and also acutely aware of the problems that a mixed-race couple could encounter. She refused to enter situations where she and Roy could be subject to racist abuse. To avoid being insulted when they went to the cinema, the couple would arrive just as the lights were lowered for the start of the film and leave as the credits rolled before the lights came up again. Although her mother Rachel initially expressed doubts about the relationship, Roy was welcomed into the Austin family. 'That must have been a very brave thing to do,' Geoff Francis, the son whose conception had precipitated Roy and Rene's rushed marriage, would say 80 years later. In fact, Geoff being conceived out of wedlock was the only social stigma felt by the couple. For years Roy and Rene added an extra year to their wedding anniversary to hide the fact that Geoff had been conceived before they were wed, a reflection of the deep sense of shame which illegitimacy still caused.

WHEN HARRY MET ROY

Roy's prospects took a turn upwards at the opening of the 1938–39 season. He was selected to play at left centre three-quarter in the first team's opening match of the new season against Wakefield Trinity.

He played well and scored a try in a 15-10 win. But he was replaced for the next match by the experienced England international Jack Garvey, a robust stand-off who had been moved into the centre position to bolster its size and aggression. Still only 19, Roy had to wait almost two months to get another chance in the first team, when he was moved out to play on the left wing in a 15-5 defeat at Halifax. He then played the next two matches against Leeds and Oldham out on the wing. Although he didn't know it at the time, his last match in a Wigan shirt was on 3 December at Oldham. The slow but steady career path mapped out for him by the club was to be overturned suddenly by a change of regime at Central Park.

In October 1939, Harry Sunderland arrived in Wigan to become the secretary-manager of the club. He immediately announced he was going to restore the team to its former glory at the top of the sport, and that he was also planning for Wigan to make the first-ever club tour to Australia. At last it seemed Wigan had a manager whose ambition matched that of its fans, which was precisely why Wigan's directors had appointed him. Short, stocky and possessing a showman's swagger, Sunderland was an engine driver's son, born in 1889 in the Australian town of Gympie, 110 miles from Brisbane. After leaving school he became an apprentice printer on the *Toowoomba Chronicle* before graduating to its sports desk. As he would remain for the rest of his life, the young Harry was a restless, driven and highly ambitious man.

While making his way as a journalist, he also became a local rugby league administrator. These were exciting times in Australian rugby. Just as in England in 1895, the game had split in two in 1907, and the new rugby league code rapidly eclipsed the union game. Sunderland, always one to have an eye on the main chance, was appointed secretary of the Queensland Rugby League in 1913, making him one of the most powerful men in Australian rugby league while still in his early twenties.

Today, it is unthinkable that a sports journalist could also be a leading sports administrator, but in the early days of football and rugby it was not uncommon. In the early 1900s John Bentley combined being president of the Football League with the editorship

of the leading sports weekly *Athletic News*. Sunderland likewise saw
no contradiction in the two roles, which allowed him to be the
manager of the Australian Kangaroo touring teams to Britain in
1929, 1933 and 1937, while also reporting on those same tours for
Australian newspapers.

Nicknamed 'The Little Dictator' by his many enemies,
Sunderland was a deeply polarising figure. He was a compulsive
self-publicist who didn't just want to write the headlines, but
wanted to be in the headlines. While he was in Britain in 1922
reporting on that season's Kangaroo tour, the Queensland Rugby
League split into two rival organisations over his administration
of the game. Players set up a union and went on strike against
his handling of insurance claims, while the local Brisbane Rugby
League broke away to defend rugby league in the city from what it
saw as Sunderland's autocratic behaviour. The bad blood ran so deep
that when news broke of his possible move to Wigan emerged, the
Brisbane Rugby League sent him a telegram saying 'if you desire to
do the game a service in Queensland, suggest you accept the Wigan
offer immediately.'

Wigan had first approached Sunderland when he was managing
the 1937 Kangaroo tour to Britain. The club was in something
of a slump. Apart from winning the Championship in 1934 the
team had won nothing since 1929. It was also haemorrhaging
money, reporting a loss of £642 in 1937, which increased to £1,314
the following year. Sunderland seemed just the man to raise the
club back to its former glory. In July 1938 he announced he had
accepted the job of secretary-manager (in modern terms it would
be a combination of chief executive and director of football) and
would be moving to Wigan for the start of the 1938–39 season on a
four-year contract. His salary was an astronomical £400 a year, plus
£3 for winning a match and £1 for a draw, plus 10 per cent of the
club's annual profits. By way of contrast, a Wigan miner's average
annual wage in the mid-1930s was around £125.

He eventually arrived on 24 October, 1938, after sailing from
Australia to America and then on to England on board the luxury
liner, the *Queen Mary*. He could not have picked a better time to set

foot in Wigan. The previous Saturday the team won the Lancashire Cup against a heavily fancied Salford team, and hundreds of fans turned out at Central Park to see the trophy and welcome the new manager. This would also be the first time that Roy Francis met Harry Sunderland, as testified to by a newspaper photograph of Jim Sullivan holding the Lancashire Cup for Sunderland to inspect while Roy looks on. What, if anything, Sunderland said to Roy is not recorded.

We can surmise very little was said. After Sunderland became manager, Roy played just three more first-team matches. He was put on the transfer list on 6 January and transferred eight days later for £450. Less than three months after Sunderland's arrival, Roy was running out at Central Park, not in the cherry and white of Wigan, but in the blue and white of Barrow.

ANATOMY OF A TRANSFER

Roy's transfer was not popular among Wigan fans. A letter appeared in the *Wigan Examiner* on 17 January, complaining about the move. 'Why has Francis been transferred?' the writer asked. 'Next to [Jack] Morley he was considered by hundreds [of fans] to be the best three-quarter at the club and he has not had a real chance.' The rugby league correspondent of the *Barrow News and Mail* reported that Barrow supporters were asking why Wigan had sold a player of such promise. 'I was taxed with a similar question,' he wrote on his way to see Roy make his debut for Barrow. 'Francis at twenty has many years of football in him. He is a stylist and can exploit his ability.' So what had happened to bring about such an abrupt change in fortune?

In the 1980s, Roy told the rugby league historian Robert Gate that the reason he was transferred from Wigan was because Sunderland did not like the colour of his skin. He also described to his sons how Sunderland had told him, 'I can't be doing with you.' As a black man in a white world, Roy understood instinctively the subtle signs and signals of racial prejudice. The tone of voice, the body language, the slight but telling difference in attitude; every black person develops an internal radar to guard against covert or overt racism, something which is not always apparent to those not on the receiving end. As Roy would later explain, 'racialism is like pain. It's a very, very personal thing.' When it came to Roy's transfer, racial prejudice, rather than rugby reasons, seems to have been the only logical reason.

Certainly, it made little sense from a team-building perspective. Roy had been signed as a long-term prospect, so there was no point in nurturing him if another club was to benefit when he matured. Wigan's senior three-quarters, Eddie Holder, Gwyn Davis and Jack Morley, would all be in their thirties by the end of the season, whereas Roy was sold six days before his 20th birthday. Moreover, it was widely acknowledged that Wigan had a problem in the centre three-quarter position, as Sunderland himself admitted. A couple of weeks after Roy was sold, Sunderland signed London Welsh rugby union centre Ossie Jones, who ended up playing only nine first-team matches. Things got so bad that just two months after he sold Roy, Sunderland was forced to play the club's new Welsh second-rower, Gwyn Williams, as a centre three-quarter. Wigan's problem was highlighted when the *Manchester Evening News* headlined its preview of the forthcoming 1939–40 season with 'Wigan Need New Centre'.

Nor did Roy's transfer add up in a business sense. Apart from Roy, the club did not sell any major players that season and, far from using the transfer market to trade Wigan back into profitability, the club's accounts for the 1938–39 season indicate a loss of over £2,000 on transfers. In fact, Sunderland's first season as manager resulted in the club losing £2,056, bigger than any of its losses before his arrival. Disquiet about the gap between Sunderland's public pronouncements and the problems on and off the field came to a head in February 1939 when three of the club's 10 directors proposed a vote of no confidence in him. Although this was defeated, the writing was on the wall.

As Roy suspected, there seemed to be something personal in Sunderland's treatment of him. When Roy returned to play against Wigan with Barrow, Sunderland wrote in his *Brisbane Telegraph* column: 'One favourite with the fans who has been mostly in our second team, a coloured youth named Francis, was sold to Barrow ... My judgement of Francis, and our own centres I preferred to promote in front of him, proved safe enough. Francis did not make any progress, had a bad day, our centres and loose forwards saw to that, and Wigan won by seven to nil.'

This fails to mention the match was played on a rain-sodden muddy pitch, had 79 scrums, and only one try was scored. It was not a day to be a three-quarter. Nor does Sunderland refer to other players in such personal terms, and the mention of Roy's colour appears gratuitous.

But there were also other indications of Sunderland's underlying attitudes. In July 1939, two months before Germany's invasion of Poland started World War Two, Sunderland wrote an article for the *Brisbane Telegraph* about his summer holiday in Europe. Although he lamented the coming threat of war, he was full of enthusiasm about his visit to Nazi Germany. Describing Beethoven's birthplace in Bonn, he ends his paragraph by listing famous German composers and inventors, together with one contemporary politician: 'Beethoven! Hitler! Röntgen! Diesel! Wagner! How sad it is that there are not more Germans like them.' There seems to be little doubt that Roy's suspicions were correct.

Under the daily scrutiny of Wigan's highly educated rugby league public, it did not take long for Sunderland's braggadocio style to be found out. Just 11 months after his triumphant arrival, his contract was terminated in September 1939.

But by then, the world had become a very different place.

3

Life During Wartime: 1939–1945

'[In the army,] you not only had to make their bodies
right but their minds right as well. … and this, I believe,
is the basis of coaching.'

Roy signed for Barrow on 14 January, 1939. The clubs had begun negotiations just after the new year and agreed a transfer fee of £450, but the move had been delayed, partly by a last-minute bid by Warrington to lure Roy, but also by Roy's determination to drive a hard bargain with his new club. Although he wouldn't turn 20 until five days after his transfer, he already understood the first law of being a professional athlete: never undervalue yourself.

Barrow were unusual at this time in rugby league because they paid all their first-team players the same match fee. Most clubs made higher payments to star players and usually paid more to backs than to forwards, but Barrow decided in 1934 to pay all players equally. The policy had paid dividends. From being anchored in the bottom quarter of the league for most of the early 1930s, the team climbed up the table every season. In 1937–38 they had finished in the top four – five places above Wigan – and reached the Challenge Cup final at Wembley for the very first time. This was an ambitious club and Roy wanted to make sure that if he couldn't command a high wage, he would benefit in other ways.

He reached an agreement with Barrow's directors that they would find him a job, ideally one that would allow him time to play and train, but would also give him skills that would help him in life beyond rugby. They found him a job in a local gun shop, a step up from the coal delivery job he had at Wigan, and provided him with a terraced house in West View Road, a five-minute walk from the club's Craven Park ground. As if to confirm that the move was the start of a new chapter in Roy's life, on 29 January Rene gave birth to their son, Geoff.

On the pitch, things could not have started better. Roy's first appearance in Barrow's blue and white saw them sweep away last season's champions Hunslet by 20 points to 2. Playing at right centre three-quarter, he made two tries by launching long passes first to winger Val Cumberbatch and then to stand-off John Higgin. 'Sentinel', the *North-Western Daily Mail*'s rugby league correspondent, was effusive: 'I like Francis. This Welsh-born lad has good stuff in him. Equally at home at stand-off and centre, he has the build, knows the tactics and can get his man. The crowd too showed their appreciation for his smart work in no uncertain way.'

Apart from the disappointing defeat at a muddy Wigan the following week, the rest of the season was a triumph for Roy. He played in all of Barrow's remaining 18 games and scored eight tries. The club finished eighth in the league, a satisfying one place above Wigan.

Roy was not the first black player at Barrow. He wasn't even the only black player in Barrow's current team. Val Cumberbatch, the right-winger for whom Roy had created a try in the Hunslet match, was born in Liverpool in 1911 to a father from Barbados and a mother from the Isle of Man. Val's father Theo had worked as a ship's steward and settled in Liverpool, where his wife Mary gave birth to their six children. Shortly before World War One the family moved to Barrow, like thousands of others who moved to the shipbuilding boomtown to find jobs in its steelworks and shipyards. In just 50 years the town's population had grown from 4,491 in 1861 to 71,821 in 1911. Abundant natural resources, enviable coastal geography, and extensive railway links made the town the engineering centre of England's far north-west, and the rugby club – formed in 1875 by the town's upper-middle classes but soon embraced by the incoming working classes – carried the flag of local civic pride.

Around the same time as the Cumberbatch family arrived in Barrow, the club signed its first black player, Jimmy Peters. Although born in Salford, Peters came from a circus family and as a boy performed as a bare-back horse rider. When he broke his arm in a riding accident and could no longer perform, he was sent away to an orphanage. A talented all-round sportsman, he began playing rugby union for Bristol in 1900 before moving to Plymouth. In March 1906 he was picked for England in that year's Calcutta Cup match. Although England won, there was much disquiet expressed that a black man was appearing in the white of the England national team, and he was conspicuously not picked later that year to play against the South African Springbok tourists.

A shipyard carpenter, Jimmy injured his hand at work in 1909 and, believing his rugby career was over, accepted a fund-raising testimonial from Plymouth. This was against rugby union's amateur regulations and was punishable by a life ban from the sport. However, Jimmy recovered from the hand injury and resumed playing. But by this time rugby in the South West of England was in financial crisis and a number of local rugby clubs switched to play rugby league. Along with 19 other players and officials, Jimmy was banned from rugby union. Confronted with the tyranny of distance between themselves and rugby league's northern heartlands, the South-west rugby league clubs lasted barely a season. Still keen to carry on playing rugby, Jimmy signed for Barrow and made his debut in October 1913. Already approaching the twilight of his career, he played only a handful of games for his new club, and in the summer of 1914 he transferred to St Helens. Within a few weeks of his move, World War One broke out and Jimmy returned home to Plymouth, where he resumed working in the docks.

Jimmy Peters and the Cumberbatch family were part of a small but not insignificant black working-class presence in pre-World War One Britain. They could be found in the mines, the steelworks, the shipyards and all of the other important sectors of the industrial economy. And, given the centrality of sport to the culture of industrial towns and cities, they could also be found playing the games of the working classes. Val Cumberbatch and his older brother Jimmy both became professional rugby league players after taking up the sport as teenagers, Jimmy playing for St Matthew's Church and Val for Cambridge Street Old Boys. In September 1932, Jimmy signed for Broughton Rangers in Manchester and Val was signed by Barrow a month later. Despite their sporting prowess, the Cumberbatch brothers were faced with police harassment. In 1925 the then teenage brothers were fined 10 shillings for 'gambling with cards', while their elder brother Joe was sentenced to hard labour for being drunk and disorderly and refusing to leave two pubs during which he had declared 'that they were all against him'.

Jimmy and Val quickly made an impression in professional rugby league. In 1935 Jimmy was picked for Lancashire against Yorkshire, scoring a try in a performance that led the reporter to note that 'his name is now being mentioned as a candidate for the Australian tour'. The following year Val was also selected for Lancashire on the opposite wing to Jimmy, and both brothers scored a try in a 28-6 crushing of Yorkshire. It was the first time that two black Britons had ever played together in a representative team in any sport. In 1937 Jimmy was selected to play for England against France, when he scored two tries, and a year later, Val also made a try-scoring debut for England against the French. Val played almost his whole career in his hometown, while Jimmy switched from Broughton to the expansion club Newcastle in 1937, only for it to collapse under financial strain at the end of the season. He then moved to play out the rest of his career at Keighley.

Roy felt comfortable at Barrow and in his first few matches for his new club he formed an eye-catching partnership with the now-veteran Val. 'Another season, and Roy Francis is a star,' the *Barrow News* confidently told its readers. But in the first week of his second season at the club, Roy's future – and that of the entire world – was irrevocably changed.

ROY AT WAR

On Sunday 3 September, 1939, Britain declared war on Germany and World War Two began. The rugby league season was just two matches old. Roy helped Barrow win their opening match against Liverpool Stanley and then played in a 10-all draw at Widnes the day before war was declared. The Rugby Football League immediately suspended all operations and awaited instructions from the government.

Unlike at the start of World War One in 1914, the government quickly decided that professional sport should continue as a way of boosting morale and providing entertainment for the workers on the home front. So rugby league restarted on 30 September, but severe restrictions on travel meant the league was now divided into two 'Emergency Leagues', one for Lancashire and one for Yorkshire. Roy played in Barrow's first three matches, and was then called up to serve in the Royal Army Service Corps on 16 October, 1939. He was one of hundreds of thousands of men who flooded into the armed forces during the early months of the war. But in one highly significant way he was very different. Indeed, according to the letter of the law at that time, he should not have been allowed to become a British soldier at all.

In 1938 the Army Council had introduced Order 89, which specified that only men of 'pure European descent' could join the army. This brought the army into line with the Royal Air Force, which since the end of World War One had only allowed white men to enlist. The Royal Navy allowed black seamen to enlist as cooks and stewards, but even they were not eligible for pensions when they retired from the service, and only men of 'pure European descent' could become officers. This colour bar in the British armed forces came under public scrutiny in the late 1930s as the danger of war with Nazi Germany grew and advertisements for naval officers of 'pure European descent' appeared across the country. When Edinburgh's George Price was turned down by the Royal Navy and the Royal Air Force because he was black, he decided to register as a conscientious objector in protest at the discrimination he faced. This was also refused. As a letter-writer to *The Scotsman* asked, 'Is the "pure European" so much more defensible, either scientifically or morally, than the German "pure Aryan"? It rather looks as though we had anticipated Herr Hitler in the matter'.

It seems likely that Roy slipped through the colour bar because of the army's rush to recruit in the early weeks of the war. Recruitment procedures were swamped by the huge numbers wanting to join up, and Roy's status as a local sporting celebrity would have helped to ease his way into the forces. In fact, he broke the ban by just three days, because on 19 October the government announced that 'during the present emergency' the colour bar would be lifted in the armed forces and non-white servicemen would be eligible for 'emergency' promotions to officer. Even so, the suspension of the colour bar during the war did not mean it did not still exist informally, as one civil servant in the Colonial Office admitted: 'This does not, of course, mean that British subjects who are obviously men of colour will in practice receive commissions.'

Roy's experience of driving a coal lorry in Wigan was enough to get him posted to the Royal Army Service Corps (RASC) as a motor mechanic and driver. He was sent to Bulford Camp, a large army training centre on Salisbury Plain in Wiltshire, and was stationed there until December 1941 as a member of No. 3 Training Battalion (Drivers) of the RASC. The RASC was responsible for the army's supply chains, transporting everything from food supplies to heavy armoury around the world, and Roy would eventually graduate to driving tank transporter lorries. Even at this point his leadership qualities were apparent. Two days after his 21st birthday he was promoted to the rank of lance-corporal. Two months after that, he was made a corporal, and in June 1940 he became a sergeant, making him quite possibly the only black British non-commissioned officer in the British Army at that time. Even so, it is striking that, unlike almost all of those he served alongside, Roy never received an overseas posting: a black man in a position of authority was an example the authorities did not want to show to troops from the British colonies.

Roy was happy working in the South of England. Rene and baby Geoff moved to Wiltshire to be near him and on 20 September, 1941, Rene gave birth to another baby boy, Ian, in Aldershot General Hospital. There was just one great absence in his life. By the time Ian was born, Roy had not played a game of competitive rugby since Barrow lost at Widnes on Boxing Day 1939. Wartime restrictions on travel meant it was almost as difficult as it was arduous to travel the 200 or so miles back north to play in a match. Eventually, 16 months after his last match, Roy travelled up to Dewsbury in April 1941 to be a guest player in the club's game against Oldham. His journey was something of a route march. He walked from Bulford army camp to Salisbury railway station, 'Then by delayed train to suburban London, by motorbike into London, truck to the station, and finally by train to Dewsbury. Almost 15 hours one way!' he later remembered. It was worth it though, as he scored a try in Dewsbury's 13-9 win. His appetite whetted, Roy now craved more competitive rugby.

RUGBY DURING WARTIME

Roy's choice of Dewsbury to rekindle his career may seem strange. The club had only finished in the top half of the table twice in the 1930s and were next to bottom of the league in the last season before the war. For a player aiming for the highest honours, Dewsbury was not a first-choice club. But the war radically altered the sporting landscape. The rugby league authorities suspended all player contracts for the duration of the war and allowed players to turn out as 'guest' players for other clubs. This new freedom was introduced because of wartime travel difficulties and to reduce costs for clubs. A maximum wage of 25 shillings (£1.25) per match was also mandated. Although these new regulations seemed to equalise the burden on clubs, unscrupulous club officials quickly spotted loopholes which could be exploited in their own club's interests.

Perhaps the most devious, and certainly the cleverest, of those officials was Dewsbury's Eddie Waring. Born and bred in the town, Eddie was a trained journalist and a successful youth rugby league coach who became the secretary-manager of Dewsbury in 1936, aged just 25. But with low crowds and even less money, even the energetic and innovative Waring struggled to resuscitate the ailing club. Until, that is, war broke out. The town was transformed overnight, as the nearby Caulms Wood army camp ballooned in size and the local woollen factories were inundated with orders for military uniforms. For the club, crowds increased while the new rugby league payment regulations meant costs decreased. Eddie realised that now players could 'guest' for other clubs, there was nothing to stop him bringing the game's best players to Dewsbury. In total, Roy was just one of 72 guest players Eddie recruited between 1940 and 1942.

Questions were inevitably asked about how Dewsbury was able to attract so many players. Most notoriously, Wigan complained to the RFL that their great fullback Jim Sullivan had decided to play for Dewsbury despite the fact he lived in Wigan. They had offered him the maximum 25 shillings, yet he still opted to make a round trip of 120 miles to turn out for Dewsbury. How, Wigan wondered, could he afford the travel costs if Dewsbury were also paying him no more than the mandated 25 shillings? The answer of course was that Dewsbury paid him an illegal extra amount. This also explained how the club could attract not only Jim Sullivan, but also Lions tourists Alan Edwards, Eric Batten, Barney Hudson and George Curran, not to mention Australian tourist Vic Hey and Great Britain captain Gus Risman.

Roy had learned the art of negotiation from his dealings with Wigan and Barrow, and would have made sure he benefited financially from his arrangement with Eddie Waring. The two also became close friends for a time, and Eddie was godfather to Roy's younger son Ian. Until the two families drifted apart after the end of World War Two, Eddie was a doting godfather to Ian, who later remembered that when he was born, 'Eddie said to my mum, when he's one, I'll give him a quid. When he's two, I'll give him three quid. When he's three, six quid, and so on and so on. But when I was four, he realised what he'd done and packed it in!' The fact that the notoriously money-conscious Waring let his godfatherly feelings overwhelm his usual financial astuteness says much about the closeness of the two families at that time.

But perhaps the biggest benefit of signing for Dewsbury was that it gave Roy the chance to play alongside some of the greatest three-quarters in rugby league history. In his first full season with Dewsbury he finished the season as rugby league's top try-scorer with 30 tries. Dewsbury also finished top of the league and were crowned champions. To cap a wonderful season, Roy was also selected for his first representative match, making a try-scoring debut for the Army's victorious Northern Command team against a Rugby League XIII. Eighty years later, rugby league administrator Roland Davis could still remember the thrill of standing on the terraces with his father and watching Roy on the wing: 'I remember going over to Dewsbury and seeing Roy Francis playing. He was so fast! I can still see him, going down the slope and no one could catch him. He scored some spectacular tries. He was such a good player.' The judgement of eight-year-old Davis was shared by those of more advanced years. 'Even the great Brian Bevan would have met his equal in Francis of those war years. He had everything – speed, swerve, side-step and guts. He and Bevan are the outstanding wingmen of the last 10 years,' recalled a Dewsbury journalist in the 1950s.

None of this could have happened had Roy not been transferred to the RASC's No 3 Tank Transporter Company in Yorkshire early in September 1941. His job was driving the large trucks which ferried tanks up and down the country. Stationed at first in York and then conveniently in Dewsbury, Roy's military duties barely interfered with rugby and he played in 29 of Dewsbury's 33 games that season. To be transferred to the town in which he played his rugby league would appear to be a coincidence of almost unimaginable good fortune, and it is difficult to imagine it happened without strings being pulled behind the scenes. Given the passing of time, we can never be sure what happened, but many commanding officers sought out famous athletes to sprinkle sporting stardust on their operations and bolster the morale of the troops under their command.

In April 1942, Roy was accepted onto a three-week course
on 'Physical & Recreation Training' at the Army's Northern
Command School of Physical Training in Bradford. In July he
went on another course and was so successful that a month later he
was seconded to undergo training at the Army Physical Training
School in Aldershot. On 19 September he was permanently
transferred from the RASC to the Army Physical Training Corps
(APTC) at Strensall near York. After almost three years as an army
driver, he was now a 'Sergeant Instructor' teaching military fitness
to combat troops.

Taking three years to be accepted by the APTC was a long time
for a soldier in World War Two. Roy's friend Trevor Foster, the
Welsh forward who built a career at Bradford Northern, applied
and was accepted three months after being called up in 1940. For
famous soccer players, the transition could be even quicker. Joe
Mercer, the Everton and Arsenal half-back who later managed
Manchester City, joined the Royal Artillery on 18 September,
1939 and was transferred to the APTC 11 days later. At 23 years
old, Roy was younger than Foster and Mercer and not as famous
as either, but the fact that he was a professional athlete and had
been promoted to sergeant within eight months of enlisting might
suggest that the long delay in being accepted by the APTC was due
to the colour of his skin.

The APTC was created in 1860 after the Crimean War revealed
the poor physical health of many British soldiers. Like rugby and
soccer, it was very much a product of the 19th century 'Muscular
Christian' belief in the moral and religious value of physical
exercise, as expressed in the saying 'a healthy mind in a healthy
body' which became APTC's official motto. By World War Two
the APTC focused on three goals: making sure all soldiers were
'fighting fit and fit to fight', providing specialist training for
military activities, and rehabilitating injured soldiers. Instructors
like Roy led new recruits through a gruelling induction process
to raise their fitness levels, and physical exercise continued as a
daily part of service life. Sport became a vital component of battle
preparation, and each form of combat has its own specific training

regime. Individual sports such as wrestling and boxing prepared troops for hand-to-hand fighting, while team sports such as soccer and rugby union were believed to 'promote comradeship and create "team spirit"'.

At the outbreak of the war, the APTC had 280 Physical Training Instructors (PTIs), a number which grew to over 3000 by 1945. Professional football and rugby players were ideally suited to be PTIs. Already physically fit, the best of them were highly disciplined, understood the value of teamwork, and possessed leadership skills. Over 100 professional soccer players became PTIs, including Joe Mercer and his teammate Frank Swift from Manchester City, Matt Busby, Bill Nicholson, future England captain Billy Wright, his Wolves teammate Stan Cullis, and England and Arsenal centre-forward Tommy Lawton. There was also a sprinkling of rugby league players such as Trevor Foster, Salford winger Alan Edwards and, eventually, Roy himself.

The long-term influence of the APTC on post-war football and rugby cannot be underestimated. A whole generation of future managers and coaches were trained in its scientific methods of physical fitness, and these former PTIs took what they had learned and applied it to professional sport in the 1940s and 1950s. The first four principles of army training as spelled out in the introduction to the APTC's *Basic and Battle Physical Training* manual were mobility, strength, endurance and 'agility, dexterity and speed', exactly what was required from soccer and rugby players. PTIs were also trained in leadership, team-building and planning skills, all of which were crucial for successful coaching careers. And serving in a leadership position in the armed forces inevitably enhanced the self-confidence and authority of those who would go on to coach in the post-war decades. It is not accidental that many of the golden generation of British soccer managers – most notably Matt Busby, Joe Mercer and Bill Nicholson – all served in the APTC.

Roy was also part of that generation, and his future coaching career was shaped by his experience in the APTC. His preparation and planning for training sessions, his use of varied activities to improve the range of his players' skills, and his acute people-management skills all originated in or were enhanced by his time in the APTC. For his son Geoff, Roy's work as a PTI defined the rest of his career: 'He was very big on handling people, their thoughts and personalities; he'd picked all this up during the war years in the APTC. He was all about rehabilitating minds as much as the physical side.' Talking to the journalist Jack McNamara in 1968, Roy explained how his coaching philosophy came directly from his wartime experiences: 'You not only had to make their bodies right but their minds right as well. ... You had to start with the brain and work down – and this, I believe, is the basis of coaching.'

Looking back a quarter of a century later, K. A. Thomas, a wounded soldier who Roy treated at Ovenden Park Convalescent Depot in Halifax, explained how he struggled on an assault course which had to be completed before he could return to his regiment. He explained he was 'among the stragglers – the special targets of Roy Francis' ability as PTI and as a dispenser of that most magical of qualities – enthusiasm. Without a word raised in anger, without a word of reproach, he urged us on by a wonderful example of encouragement and – unknown in my experience of Army PT Instructors – by the most gentlemanly of persuasive psychology, to complete the course with 30 seconds to spare! Indeed, this was the stuff of which coaches are made'. Thomas's praise of his instructor would be repeated in the same terms by dozens of men who would later be coached by Roy.

Of course, Roy differed from every other famous sportsman who passed through the ranks of the APTC. He was in all probability the first black man to have served in the APTC since its foundation. We don't know how this affected his relations with the servicemen he was training or helping to recover, almost all of whom would have been white. As with many aspects of his life, he doesn't appear to have talked about this with his family or friends. The one overt example of discrimination he spoke about happened in 1942 when he and the family were still living at Bulford training camp. Rene entered their youngest son Ian in a 'beautiful baby' competition. Ian won, but then the judges decided they couldn't have a mixed-race child as the winner and took the first prize away from him.

To have been a black person leading white people was a highly unusual situation in Britain. Other than Roy, the only written record of this happening in World War Two is from Ita Ekpenyon, a Nigerian teacher and actor who worked as a Senior Air Raid Precaution Warden in London during the height of the Blitz in 1940 and 1941. Ekpenyon certainly encountered racism. He recalled being regarded as a lucky omen because he was black, and also what he described as 'uneasiness' when he had to bodily shield a white woman from a bomb blast. He occasionally found people reluctant to follow his orders, including once when occupants of an air-raid shelter tried to stop non-British people coming in, but on the whole he found his authority was largely accepted by those in his charge. This was probably similar to the situation Roy faced with the soldiers for whom he was responsible.

Even so, his career with the APTC was strangely limited. According to army records, he was based at the Strensall Camp near York for a time, and from July 1944 lived at home while he was posted temporarily to military hospitals in Lincoln and Askham Bryan near York to rehabilitate wounded soldiers, before being permanently based at an army convalescent camp at Ovenden near Halifax. His most exotic posting was a secret three-month stint in Whitby during the summer of 1944, where he helped train Royal Artillery drivers in how to drive communications lorries and operate radios in preparation for the D-Day invasion. Roy's purely domestic army career differed sharply from those of other rugby league-playing soldiers such as Trevor Foster, who travelled to France and across the Middle East, and Gus Risman, who was also posted abroad and spent time in Algiers, not to mention the APTC's soccer players' extensive overseas postings. Of course, Roy's more well-travelled comrades were not men of colour, and so did not suffer the consequences of the British authorities' belief that black men in positions of authority might cause colonial troops to question the racial hierarchy of the British Empire.

THE WELSH ENGLISHMAN

The year 1942 was the breakout year for Roy's rugby league career. Aged 23, he was the game's top try-scorer, a league championship winner with Dewsbury, and a recognised representative player. He was a certainty for the Welsh rugby league team to play against England in February 1943, until something unique in rugby history happened.

Two months after war was declared, the Rugby Football Union lifted its ban on rugby league players playing for military rugby union teams. In 1895, the RFU had barred any league player, amateur or professional, from playing union for life. The ban had been lifted for the last two years of World War One before being reimposed. The inter-war years saw numerous players banned from union for the crime of having played in a game of league or, in some cases, merely having met with league officials. But in World War Two the RFU's attitude went against the spirit of 'national unity' and it quickly lifted its ban for servicemen, although not for civilian rugby league players.

The lifting of the ban was also an opportunity for rugby union to select famous league players for its representative sides. By the start of 1943 Roy was one of the hottest properties in rugby, and in February he was simultaneously picked to play on the same day for Wales at league and for England in a services union international against Scotland. Roy had no choice in which match he played. Rugby union's status meant that it automatically took priority over rugby league. He had no say in the nation for which he played either. His fellow Welshman and close friend, Bradford's Trevor Foster, remembered that, 'A Major Sloane was the officer in charge of rugby union and he picked Roy on the wing for England. When Roy told him he was Welsh, Sloane said "never mind" and that was that.'

That a Welsh rugby league player could be selected for what was effectively the England national team highlighted the flexibility of wartime rugby union. It also raised the question of why Roy was not picked by the Welsh rugby union selectors for their services international team. They regularly included Welsh league players and the side was at one point captained by Gus Risman. Perhaps the prejudice which kept black players out of the Wales national rugby union team until the 1980s was also at work during wartime.

Donning the white shirt of England, Roy made a try-scoring debut in a sweeping 29-6 defeat of Scotland in Edinburgh, one of five tries and four conversions scored by the team's quartet of rugby league players. Scotland had won the previous two meetings between the sides but, as the *Scotsman* noted, 'England had introduced fresh blood from the Rugby League and the invigorating effect of the infusion was manifest'. Roy made two other tries and the *Scotsman* went on to ruefully note that 'the gracefully swift, deceptive running of Francis had a disturbing influence on the Scottish defenders'. He scored five more tries in the other six England internationals he played over the next 14 months.

Even being one of the stars of the England team was not enough to protect him from racial prejudice. Two months after his England debut, Roy was picked for the return match against Scotland at Leicester's Welford Road ground. He travelled down by train from Yorkshire and arrived at the ground a couple of hours before the 3 p.m. kick-off. Historian John Schleppi documented what then happened to Roy:

> 'He encountered the two elderly gentlemen who enquired, "What do you want?" "I would like to go into the grounds," replied Francis. "We don't open until 2pm," explained the two. Francis tried again. "But I've travelled a long way and would like to rest in the dressing room." Surprised, they responded, "What do you want to be in the dressing room for?" "I'm playing for England!" Francis exclaimed. Whereupon one gentleman turned to the other, leaning against the wall in disbelief and with peals of laughter said, "Hey, Charlie, this is playing for England!" It was only after nearly one and one-half hours and the persistence of the England manager that Francis was admitted to the ground.'

Suffering such humiliation made little difference to Roy's performance that afternoon. After 25 minutes he had to switch from the wing to the centre position to replace Wigan's Johnny Lawrenson, who went off with a cracked rib. Playing with just 14 men, England ran out 24-19 winners, with Roy strolling away from the Scottish defenders to score the last and game-sealing try. The following year he scored the 'prettiest try of the match' in England's only wartime victory over Wales. In all he appeared in seven of England's 16 service internationals, making him the fourth most capped British or Irish player of World War Two.

As if being a Welshman playing for England and the first black athlete to play international rugby union in England since 1908 was not enough, Roy also appeared in a unique pair of cross-code games when rugby league teams played rugby union sides. In January 1943, the Northern Command Sports Board arranged a match between a Northern Command Rugby League XV and a Northern Command Rugby Union XV at Headingley under rugby union rules. Roy played for the league side which won 18-11 after trailing 8-3 at half-time. The match was such a success that another was staged in Bradford 15 months later, again using union rules. This was a much more representative affair with both Combined Services teams drawn from the army, navy, and air force. Once again, the league side trailed at half-time before staging a late comeback, winning in the final minutes thanks to a scrum move when stand-off Stan Brogden exchanged passes with Roy to scorch away to score the match-winning try. As an indicator of the social differences between the two versions of rugby, the union teams were packed with officers but both league squads consisted entirely of the 'other ranks'. Just as tellingly, no black player would emulate Roy's feat of playing at the highest levels of British rugby union for another 40 years.

The second cross-code match turned out to be Roy's last major game of the war. In July 1944, while stationed at Whitby, he broke a leg and tore his ligaments, resulting in a lengthy stay at Hemlington Hospital on the outskirts of Middlesbrough. Although his army record stated that these were 'accidental injuries of a trivial nature', the impact on his rugby career was enormous. There are no records of how long it took him to recover or if any complications occurred, although Roy told an interviewer in 1957 that the doctors had at one point told him it was the end of his playing career.

Apart from three minor army matches in the 1944–45 season, Roy didn't play any serious rugby for 16 months until September 1945, when he ran out for Barrow in their first peace-time home game since 1939. Aged 20 when war broke out, he was now almost 27. The years which in normal times would have established him at the peak of his powers had been sacrificed to the war. And the lost season of 1944–45 had removed him from public view just as sport was preparing to return to normality. The season which the *Barrow News* predicted would make him a star was yet to come.

4

The 1946 Lions Tour and Beyond:
1945–1949

*'I was fortunate to realise my ambition and in
a way improve on it.'*

Five days before Christmas Day 1947, Roy received rugby league's highest accolade. He was selected to play for Great Britain in the third and deciding match against the touring New Zealand team. 'Well, Roy, this is it,' he was told by the hugely experienced Ernest Ward as they lined up for the kick-off in front of 45,000 fans. 'It' turned out to be Roy's day. He touched down for the first try of the match after just eight minutes, backing up a break by full-back Martin Ryan to score in the corner. 'I was tickled pink,' he recalled. 'I was fortunate to realise my ambition and in a way improve on it.'

Later in the first half he touched down again after Ernest Ward broke through the New Zealand lines and passed to Roy to send him over for another try in the corner. At half-time Britain led 17-7, but New Zealand fought back furiously and the game swung from end to end before the referee brought the drama to a conclusion. At 25-9, Britain had secured the series in what the newspapers dubbed 'one of the most thrilling games in the Rugby League's history'. Former Rugby Football League chairman Joe Lewthwaite, who claimed to have seen every international match since 1895, declared it to be 'the best test of all'. And Roy had been at the very heart of the spectacle. He had 'stamped himself as one of the best three-quarters in the game today,' wrote one admiring journalist. 'His two tries, scored in the first 30 minutes, were really magnificent.'

But it was a Great Britain debut that Roy felt was a year too late. In November 1945, the Australian Foreign Minister H. V. Evatt had interrupted his trip to the United Nations General Assembly to meet RFL officials in Manchester to persuade them to organise a Great Britain Lions tour to Australia in the summer of 1946. Many Australians had felt abandoned by the British government during the war and Evatt was keen to re-establish the bond with what most Australians still saw as the mother country. 'The close relationship that has been built up between Australia and New Zealand and the North of England is in the nature of a history,' he told the assembled officials. 'The building up of this history ought to be resumed as soon as possible.' The RFL agreed and began preparations to send a team to Australia and New Zealand in the summer of 1946. But when the names of the touring players were announced in January 1946, Roy Francis, one of the stars of wartime rugby, was not among them.

When he spoke to the historian Robert Gate in the 1980s, Roy said he believed he had not been selected for the 1946 Lions tour because of racism. 'There were clearly not four better wings than Roy in the British game yet he was left out of the quad for political reasons,' Gate later explained in his obituary of Roy. 'Australia still operated a colour bar and the British selectors were not brave enough to push the Australians into a corner.' In fact, the story was more complicated and the discrimination much more deep-rooted.

Roy's rugby career had almost completely dried up in the last 12 months of the war. The broken leg he suffered during his posting to Whitby in the summer of 1944, coupled with the demands of his work at the Ovenden Convalescent Camp, stopped him playing any rugby league matches during the 1944–45 season. He did not play in any significant rugby union games either. He lost an entire season in his mid-twenties, precisely the point where he should have been able to claim the position as the game's leading winger.

When he returned to play for Barrow in September 1945, he only managed to score three tries before the shortlist of candidates for the Lions squad was announced on 2 January, 1946. In contrast, his Barrow teammate Jim Lewthwaite scored 16 tries in the same period. Although Roy scored another 13 tries in the second half of the season, it was too late to put himself in contention when the final Lions squad was named on 11 March. As if to underline his plight, he was not even among that season's top 25 try scorers.

It seems an open-and-shut case that Roy's form was not good enough for him to be picked for the Lions tour. He was enough of a realist to understand the harsh mechanics of team selection and it is unlikely he overestimated his form. So perhaps he was referring to something else when he spoke to Gate? His statement about racism was not that his performances had been good enough to earn selection for the 1946 Lions tour, but that the colour of his skin meant that he *could not and would not* have been selected, no matter how well he was playing. There is strong and persuasive evidence to suggest that Roy fully understood that there was an unwritten colour bar that prevented black players from playing for Great Britain against Australia. To understand how this colour bar operated, we have to go back more than a decade and look at the career of Roy's former Wigan teammate, George Bennett.

THE WHITE AUSTRALIA WHITEWASH

The 1935–36 season was perhaps the most memorable of George Bennett's career. He made his international debut in Wales' first ever-match against France, and then scored the two decisive tries which defeated England to crown Wales as European Champions for the first time. For Wigan that season he played 41 matches, scored 14 tries and guided them to fourth place in the league. Tom Moores, an Australian journalist and brother of the former Leeds captain Jeff Moores, described Bennett as 'the cleverest half-back in England ... he has a sidestep, change of pace, fend, short kick, grubber, in fact every trick of the class five-eighth [as Australians called the stand-off position] ... in defence he has no superiors'. The authoritative Bradford reporter George Thomson described Bennett as 'one of the finest outside half backs we have had in the game for many years'. It seemed inevitable that his season of seasons would culminate in selection for the 1936 Lions tour to Australia and New Zealand.

In January 1936, the teams were announced for the two trial matches from which the Lions would be chosen, but George Bennett's name was not among the four stand-offs selected. The form of Salford star Emlyn Watkins made him a certainty for the Lions, but of the other three – Tommy Shaddon, Dennis Madden, and Gurnos Rees – only Madden would ever play international rugby, and that was as a centre three-quarter. None would ever play for the Lions. In fact, Watkins was the only recognised stand-off selected in the 1936 Lions' touring party, with the other stand-off place going to the supremely gifted Stan Brogden, who was primarily a three-quarter but who, according to the *Halifax Courier*, had not lived up to his reputation that season. No serious observer of the game could deny that George Bennett was one of the four best stand-offs in the game.

The British press did not mention Bennett's omission from the Lions team. It was left to Australian journalists to reveal that Bennett had been left out of the team because of his colour. Just before the touring party was announced in March, Brisbane's *Daily Standard* published an article by Tom Moores headlined 'Prejudice against Colour may keep out Brilliant Bennett'. He warned that: 'Bennett has to overcome the subtle propaganda of "colour", but if players are selected on merit, then Bennett is as big a certainty for five-eighth as Jim Sullivan is for full back.' Three days later the paper reported the announcement of the Lions squad under the headline 'Colour Deprived Bennett of Tour' saying that 'despite reassurances from Australia, the League administration decided not to risk criticism by his inclusion. It is generally opined that Bennett is the best five-eighth produced by the Rugby League'. In New Zealand, where the Lions would visit after the Australian leg of the tour, the *Auckland Star* announced the squad with the headline 'Colour Line in Rugby League'.

The Australian press were united in stressing that Bennett's exclusion was entirely the decision of the British selectors and had nothing to do with Australia's 'White Australia' policy, which banned non-white immigration and removed civil rights from Indigenous Australians. It was widely reported that the Australian rugby league authorities had not raised any objections to Bennett, with *Australian Worker* explaining that 'the colour question would not be likely to arise here in connection with the member of a sporting team, for we had the West Indies [cricket] team here a few years back. Most of them were coloured, and no exception was taken to them because of that'.

None of this was reported by British journalists, almost all of whom observed a discreet silence about Bennett's exclusion, although George Thomson did raise the issue in the *Yorkshire Observer* in January 1936: 'The colour bar is a difficult one. Never before has the Rugby League included in its touring ranks a player of this description [sic]. While we in this country may be inclined to ponder what would be the thoughts of Australians if such a player were chosen to go with the tour party, should this really be made a point at issue?'

Things were further complicated by the selection of Jimmy Cumberbatch in the two trial games from which the Lions would be selected. This led the *Halifax Courier* to suggest the selectors seemed to be free of colour prejudice, although its reporter also asked why Bennett had been excluded.

It was a good question. Selection committees were notorious for horse-trading between selectors, which often resulted in good players being overlooked. But this was not the case with Bennett, whose club Wigan had only two players in the two trial games. Moreover, there was a plethora of great wingers available to the selectors – including Jack Morley, Alan Edwards, Barney Hudson, Stan Smith and the multi-skilled Brogden – so there was little chance that Cumberbatch would be picked to tour. It seems logical to suggest that the selectors picked him to play in the tour trial matches while knowing full well he would not be selected for the tour in order to deflect any criticism that racism lay behind their exclusion of Bennett.

It is a conceit of 21st-century sport to think opposition to racism is a recent phenomenon and that previous generations were not as enlightened as today. However, this is a mistaken assumption. In 1936 there was probably more discussion about racism in sport than at any time before the 1960s. George Bennett's exclusion took place at the same time as the rise of boxer Joe Louis, who would become the second black world heavyweight champion in June 1937. It also coincided with the campaign to boycott the 1936 Berlin Olympics, and a continuing debate about the colour bar in British boxing. The Nazi regime's persecution of Jews also made racism a topic of everyday discussion. So rugby league's selectors would have been very aware of how their exclusion of Bennett from the Lions squad would be perceived.

Eighteen months later the journalist George Thomson revealed that 'certain members' of the international selection committee were 'not inclined' to select black players. In 1936, he admitted, 'Emlyn Jenkins and George Bennett were then the two best outside half-backs in the English game. Jenkins made the trip; Bennett, as Welshman of colour, was not chosen, mainly I believe because of his colour.'

This revelation came during the selection of the team to play against the Australian Kangaroo tourists in the final Test match of their 1937 tour. Incumbent loose-forward Harry Beverley suffered an attack of food poisoning a fortnight before the match and was doubtful to play. One obvious replacement was Oldham's Alec Givvons, which once again raised the question of racist selection policy. 'Colour Problem for Final Rugby League Test' was the *Yorkshire Observer*'s headline for a George Thomson article which asked 'whether [the selectors] will agree to the choice in their team of a coloured player?' There was, stated Thomson, a group of selectors who would not select Givvons 'because of his colour and the possible thoughts that may arise were he to be chosen'. A day later the selectors were saved from making that choice when Beverley announced that he had recovered and would play in the match.

The harsh reality was that until the 1950s black players could play at all levels of rugby league except in international matches against Australia. This policy does not seem to have been requested by the Australians and black players turned out as usual for their clubs in matches against Australian touring teams. It was the choice of British selectors, who hid their prejudices behind the excuse of the White Australia policy; in a similar way, the British boxing authorities justified their colour bar by claiming they had no choice if they wanted to maintain sporting relations with South Africa. George Bennett's experience in 1936 resembled the polite hypocrisy of the genteel drawing rooms of middle-class England much more than it did the straight-talking meritocracy upon which the industrial north supposedly prided itself. It was his knowledge of the 1930s that led Roy to say that his colour excluded him from the 1946 Lions tour – because regardless of form, fitness or fame, no black player would or could have been selected to tour Australia at that time. It may not have been coincidental that Roy's eventual selection for Great Britain in 1947 came soon after the colour bar had been permanently lifted in the armed forces and in boxing. Even so, it would not be until 1954 that a black player was picked to tour Australia, and even then it took the peerless Billy Boston to achieve it.

BACK TO BARROW

Although the demobilisation of British troops began in June 1945, PTIs involved in the convalescence and rehabilitation of injured soldiers continued their duties for some time, and Roy wasn't formally discharged from the army until 16 April, 1946. He was able to play in only 12 of Barrow's first 21 matches in the 1945–46 season. His most memorable moment was kicking a long-range drop goal against Warrington, which 'sailed over the cross bar at Craven Park, propelled from the angle between the touchline and the half-way line,' recalled the historian Bill Mandle almost 35 years later, evoking his schoolboy days watching Barrow with such relish that he wished 'every child [could have] so richly coloured a rite of passage'.

It was only in the last third of the season that Roy's form improved and he was picked for Wales to play France in Bordeaux. Amazingly, it was his first appearance for the Welsh national rugby league team – during the war he had been ruled out of playing league internationals because of his duties for the England rugby union services' side.

The following season saw a full return to his wartime form. He scored 28 tries in 33 Barrow matches, one in his two matches for the Welsh national side, and finished as the season's fourth highest try-scorer. This was not an inconsiderable achievement as Barrow had slipped down the league ladder to finish 12th and were knocked out in the first rounds of the cup competitions. The club was in something of a tail-spin and finished 21st of 28 clubs in the league in the 1947–48 season.

Unsurprisingly, Roy was becoming frustrated at Barrow. As the club's fortunes were declining, he himself was maturing. He had signed for Barrow as a teenager but was now a 27-year-old married man with two sons. For most of the war he had been stationed in West Yorkshire, and the travelling between Barrow and his billet at the Ovenden Convalescent Camp near Halifax, and then from his home in Wigan after he left the army, was tiring and burdensome. As he approached 30, he needed to start thinking about what he was going to do after he finished playing. In March 1946, a few days before he left for France with the Welsh national side, he put in a transfer request to leave Barrow.

He told reporters that he would prefer to play for a club in Yorkshire, and there was no lack of interest in him. In Dewsbury, local supporter Willie Mann announced a fund-raising campaign for £750 to bring him back to the club he had graced between 1941 and 1944. But, this was more a measure of the admiration of Dewsbury supporters than a serious proposal. Barrow wanted a transfer fee of £2,000 and Roy knew the value of his services, but no club was prepared to pay a large transfer fee and meet his personal demands. Only two rugby league players had ever been transferred for £2,000 or more, although in January 1949 the blazingly-quick Stan McCormick would set a new record when he moved from Manchester's Belle Vue Rangers to St Helens for a blockbusting £4,000.

By the time Roy made his debut for Great Britain in December 1947, he was living in Wigan next door to Rene's widowed but now remarried mother. After being demobbed, he returned to his old job as a coal-lorry driver. At weekends he would take six-year-old Geoff with him: 'The only thing I can remember was that we had pop bottles full of cold tea. When I came back home I had to have a bath because it was so dirty and dusty. I thought it was wonderful.' But Roy's ambitions were bigger and he took over a men's clothing shop specialising in school uniforms in Wigan's Edward Street. This provided a secure business for the future and reduced the time it took him to get to Barrow for matches, but it was still a train journey of around an hour and three-quarters, mostly undertaken in the winter.

Moreover, running the shop consumed all of Rene's time and what little Roy had left over after rugby. Although their two sons were still in infant school, they had to pick up some of the burden of household duties: 'When Ian and I got home from school, we'd make the fire, set the table for tea and to be ready for when my mother would come home from work,' remembered Geoff Francis. On the other hand, it provided a settled family life after the uncertainties of wartime. Roy's mother Rebecca travelled from Brynmawr to Wigan to stay with them for a time and left her grandsons with warm memories. 'Oh boy!' recalled Ian. 'She was Mrs Five-By-Five, as tall as she was wide. She had a ground-shaking laugh, she was always jolly.' She was also proud of her son's achievements, and would sometimes tell complete strangers that she was the mother of the famous rugby star.

In March 1948, two years after his original transfer request, Roy once again asked Barrow to put him on the transfer list. Although the size of the transfer fee was not released to the press, word leaked out that it was again £2,000. Roy complained it was too high and a deterrent to interested clubs, and the RFL forced Barrow to reduce it to £1,250. This led to the ambitious Hunslet club offering to pay the transfer fee in full, but the Hunslet directors refused to agree to Roy's personal terms. These aren't recorded, but we can assume Roy not only wanted substantial match payments but also the club's help in finding a long-term business for when his playing days ended. He had also made it known he wanted to move into coaching and that he would prefer to join a club as a player-coach. He had already led the Great Britain team in a training session in 1947, and his reputation as a leader on and off the field was well-known throughout the game.

The negotiations with Hunslet eventually broke down and Warrington stepped in to sign Roy on 11 July, 1948. Four months earlier the club had signed Barrow's outstanding Australian second-row forward Harry Bath, ripping away the cornerstone of Barrow's pack and sending out a signal to the rest of the league. No doubt this helped to smooth the way for Roy to make the same move. The personal terms of Roy's transfer were not disclosed but moving to Warrington, just 15 miles from his home in Wigan, meant he could continue running his clothes shop. Although there was no coaching position for him, the ease of travel and Warrington's growing status as a powerhouse in the sport meant that his ultimate ambition could, at least in the short term, wait.

LIFE WITH THE WIRE

The long hot summer of 1948 was a moment of change not just for Roy but for the whole of British society. The week before moving to Warrington, the new National Health Service had been officially opened, a centrepiece of the Labour government's programme of nationalisation and restructuring of the economy. On 22 June the *Empire Windrush* sailed into Tilbury Docks, bringing 800 people from the Caribbean to start new lives and ultimately change the face of Britain. The *Windrush* came to symbolise the start of a new era of immigration. By 1951 there were 15,000 West Indian-born people living in Britain. Ten years later, the 1961 Census recorded that this number had grown to 172,000.

The growth of Britain's black population had little direct impact on Roy. Most West Indians initially settled in the big cities and few came to Warrington. Even so, the town had its own history of race relations. In 1943 it had attracted national attention when the Casino Club, a dance hall specialising in jazz music, found itself under pressure from the US Army to introduce a colour bar. There was a US air base nearby at Burtonwood, and the US military enforced an unyielding policy of racial segregation between black and white personnel. When white American GIs objected one night to the presence of Herbert Greaves, a West Indian worker in a local munitions factory, the Casino's owner Nat Bookbinder told them that if they didn't like it, they could go elsewhere. 'I refused to turn Herbert out,' Bookbinder later said. 'I told him that so long as he paid his admission money, the doors would be open to him and he would be welcome.' The US Army then boycotted the club and the local Conservative MP raised the matter in Parliament. In response, the War Office said it did not support segregation but then declared the club 'out of bounds' to all British military personnel, ostensibly because of the danger of 'overcrowding'. Nat Bookbinder was then called up into the army, leaving him in the impossible situation of not being able to enter his own club.

Black American soldiers continued to be based in Burtonwood well into the 1950s and relationships between them and local white women meant there was a small community of women with mixed-race babies in the area. Even in a town such as Warrington, the mistaken idea that working-class communities were entirely white was undermined by the presence of what the historian Lucy Bland has described as 'brown babies' and by the prominence of Roy Francis in its rugby team, which was also the highest-profile representative of local civic pride.

That local pride was enhanced by the success of 'the Wire', as the team was nicknamed in honour of the town's wire-manufacturing industry. In 1947 the club finished fifth in the league, and then won the Championship for the very first time the following year.

Roy joined them just a few weeks after this success, confident that this was a team going places, even though he was not guaranteed automatic selection in the first team. On the right wing was the incomparable Brian Bevan, a balding, bony Australian winger who looked no more an athlete than Charlie Chaplin looked like an aristocrat, yet whose 796 tries were more than were scored by anyone else who ever played rugby. On the other wing was Albert Johnson, an England international who went on the 1946 Great Britain tour to Australia. Given his age, most observers thought that Roy would be what is now called a squad player without a regular place. But he forced his way into the side, playing 29 matches and scoring 22 tries, finishing as the club's second-highest try-scorer after the prodigious Bevan's 56.

Warrington went through the first half of the season unbeaten in the league and didn't lose until they went to Workington on 15 January, 1949. Excitement built as the club seemed to be rushing inexorably to a second Championship title. They finished the season at the top of the league, entitling them to a home match in the Championship semi-finals. Ironically, it was against Barrow, whose star had seemed to be waning when Roy left the previous year. He was one of the try-scorers as his old club was imperiously pushed aside by 23 points to 8. Now, at the age of 30, Roy was about to play in his first peace-time final.

Warrington's opponents were Huddersfield, a team which swept into third place in the league thanks to a try-scoring strike-force led by their trio of Australian backs, Johnny Hunter, Pat Devery and Lionel Cooper. The clash between arguably the two most attractive clubs in the league led to enormous interest in the championship showdown, and a record-breaking 75,194 spectators assembled at Manchester City's Maine Road ground to experience the drama first-hand. Fifteen special trains and 200 buses took 15,000 Warrington supporters the 20-odd miles to the stadium, every one of them fully expecting a repeat of the previous season's Championship win.

The drama began even before the ball was kicked off. Due to an administrative error, the referee failed to turn up, and the final had to be refereed by one of the touch judges, Matthew Coates, who had never previously refereed at this level. His lack of experience was not noticed during the match, which began as an intense physical confrontation as both teams vied to take control of the game. With 15 minutes gone and Huddersfield starting to impose themselves, Roy fumbled the ball near his own line, Huddersfield's Irish forward Jack Daly recovered it, and a couple of tackles later, received the ball again and scored between the Warrington posts. The initiative then swung to Warrington, who pressed the Huddersfield line but were unable to break it. As so often happens when one side pressures for too long, Warrington let their concentration drop just before half-time, and Huddersfield got the ball back and clever passing freed up Lionel Cooper to power past Brian Bevan and score in the corner.

The half-time 8-0 deficit became even worse when midway through the second half Pat Devery pounced on a kick-through and scored another try between the posts to put Huddersfield 13-0 up. But with just five minutes left in the match, Roy made a dash for the corner and under a tangle of players was awarded a try, although some reporters believed the ball had been forced from his hands before he touched down. Harry Bath converted from the touchline, and then with just two minutes remaining, Warrington then touched down again and Bath converted to make the score a nerve-jangling 13-12. But it was too late, and when Mr Coates blew the whistle to end the final he was not supposed to referee, no one could argue that Huddersfield weren't the better side.

It was the most important game of Roy's club career, on the big stage where he always wanted to play. But he would be 31 years old at his next birthday and the chances of playing again at this level were fading. He played in eight of Warrington's first 15 matches of the 1949–50 season before being dropped after the club's sixth loss of the season, despite the press noting that he played well in the match. Realising that Warrington could now offer only limited opportunities, he submitted a transfer request. On 8 November he was put on the transfer list as 'open to offers'. Warrington made it clear it wanted a four-figure sum for his signature, an outrageously high fee for a player in his thirties. But it was also an acknowledgement of the value Roy could still offer, not least in a future leadership capacity.

There was no shortage of interest. Four clubs were said to want to sign him, but it was a club on the other side of the country, Hull FC, who were most determined to make him theirs. The day after the press revealed Roy was available, Hull director Len Pattison drove over the Pennines early in the morning to discuss the transfer with the club and the player. At five o'clock terms were agreed between Hull, Warrington and Roy. The transfer fee was £1,250, the same as Warrington paid Barrow 18 months earlier, a rare example of a club not losing money on an ageing player. But, as the next decade would highlight, it was Hull and Roy Francis who ultimately profited from the deal.

LIONEL FRANCIS' FINAL ACT

By starting a new life in a new region, Roy was yet again following in his father's footsteps. In February 1941 Lionel Francis arrived in Belize City in what was then called British Honduras to take over the running of the large estate that Isaac Morter had bequeathed to the Universal Negro Improvement Association (UNIA). Just as when he had arrived in America in 1920, Lionel once again reinvented his past life in order to assist his new life. He was now known as 'Dr Lionel Francis, the Trinidadian physician' with the official title of 'Estate Manager' of the extensive Morter Estate.

The road to Belize had been a long and complex journey for Lionel, in which he had used all of considerable charm, intelligence and political skills. It began in 1926 when he rejoined the United Negro Improvement Association. Its founder Marcus Garvey was in jail for fraud and Lionel saw this as an opportunity to become one of its national leaders. But perhaps an even bigger temptation was the news that the UNIA had been named as the sole beneficiary of the considerable estate of Isaiah Morter.

Morter was a wealthy businessman in British Honduras (known as Belize since 1973), a British colony sandwiched between Mexico and Guatemala on the east coast of Central America. He became a millionaire through his ownership of a large banana and coconut plantation, and liked to style himself 'the richest black man in the world'. In 1921 he met Marcus Garvey when the UNIA was establishing a branch in British Honduras. Enthused by Garvey's politics, Morter rewrote his will in February 1924 to leave his entire estate to the UNIA. He did not tell his family.

Seven weeks later, Morter died. His widow, who had been left just 25 dollars by her husband, disputed the will and the case went all the way to the British Privy Council. In 1928 the Privy Council decided the will was valid. This was not the end of the matter, and other Morter family members took the case back to court.

By August 1929 Garvey was now out of jail and claiming that Morter's estate belonged to him. But, although Morter wanted Garvey personally to have his money, the will left the money to the UNIA, not to Garvey himself. In 1931 Lionel Francis was elected President-General of the UNIA. Under Lionel's leadership, the UNIA revealed that when its member James Hamblin asked Garvey for the return of $900 he loaned to him via the UNIA in the early 1920s, Garvey told him that he was no longer linked to the original UNIA and therefore was not responsible for its financial dealings. Inadvertently, Garvey had conceded the UNIA's right to the Morter bequest. Lionel Francis, the former miner from Brynmawr, had outwitted perhaps then the most famous black politician in the world.

He was now the undisputed leader of the UNIA. Alongside him as Assistant President-General was Henrietta Vinton Davis, a pioneering actress who was the first African American to play Shakespearean roles on the American stage. Davis had been loyal to Garvey until 1929 when she threw in her lot with Lionel. However, regardless of the outward signs of unity, the organisation was still wracked by rivalries and disputes. Despite being elected for a four-year term, Lionel's presidency lasted barely two. On 17 May, 1934 the UNIA expelled Lionel. He was accused of unspecified 'conduct unbecoming', neglect of duty, and of not carrying out his job since the previous August. In fact, he had been secretly creating a parallel organisation within the UNIA to help him capture the Morter estate for himself. He was, said UNIA secretary Julia Rumford Clark, 'crazy like a fox with his eye on the Belize legacy'.

Once again, the question of who was the beneficiary of the Morter Estate went to the courts. When the verdict was handed down, Lionel's new UNIA was named the rightful inheritor. Although his UNIA remained active in New York, its membership and activities withered. By 1940 it optimistically claimed to have 700 members across the USA. But Lionel had lost interest in it, and was now completely focused on taking control of the Morter Estate. In early 1941 he left the United States for good and sailed for British Honduras.

He made his presence felt as soon as he stepped ashore. His prominence as the manager of the Morter Estate opened many doors for him and, just a year after he arrived, he was elected onto the Belize City Council. He became the leader of what was known as the 'People's Group', which controlled the council until 1947. Like most of the West Indies at that time British Honduras was embroiled in deep-going industrial conflicts and there was also a growing movement campaigning for independence from Britain and for a 'one person, one vote' system.

But Lionel was no longer the militant politician he had been in America. Now he cultivated the image of respectable moderation, sympathetic to demands for democracy, employment rights and independence, but cautious and conservative in his approach. He became the president of the British Honduras Trades and Labour Union, and was a delegate to the 1947 Caribbean Labour Congress in Jamaica. He also represented the British Honduran government at the 1947 Montego Bay conference, an ultimately unsuccessful attempt to bring the British colonies of the Caribbean together in a Federation of the West Indies under the guidance of the British government.

As the anti-colonial and national independence movements grew stronger around the world in the 1950s, Lionel moved further away from his radical past. In 1951 he was elected as the founding chairman of the National Party, which opposed independence from Britain. Between 1952 to 1956 he served as a National Party councillor in Belize City, but his political power was waning. In 1958 the National Party was wound up and Lionel, now aged 76, went into retirement. He was persuaded back into politics early in 1961 when he was appointed the chairman of the short-lived Christian Democratic Party. This was to be his last act as a politician.

Although suffering from eye problems, he was otherwise fit and healthy until he collapsed on his way to church on Sunday 30 April, 1961. He never recovered consciousness, remained in a coma and died on Tuesday 9 May aged 80. Local newspapers remembered him as 'a colourful and very popular figure', who was 'admired for his great courage and for his tremendous services to his fellow men', and was also 'one of the best friends the people of British Honduras have ever known'.

Thus ended the remarkable and picaresque life of Lionel Francis. Did Roy inherit his father's charisma and leadership abilities? Was the son the heir to the father's gifts? Perhaps, but the roulette wheel of inheritance offers no certainties that talent will be passed between generations. More likely is the fact that Roy's mother Rebecca taught him the better qualities of her husband, such as his self-confidence, charm, and the refusal to bow down before racism. And growing up in the same Welsh society in which his father lived his first decades of adulthood meant that Roy also learned the lessons that enabled Lionel to rise so high. The personalities of both father and son were forged in a world that was collective, social and communal, and both thrived when with other people, whether it be in the chapel, the political organisation, or the rugby team. The great tragedy of their lives was that neither was aware of the other's success in creating their own worlds, or how they broke down the barriers which confronted them both.

5

The Emergence of the Master Coach:
1949–1956

'What are the basic things a coach requires?
"Knowledge, dedication, honesty and sincerity."
And what do you require from the players?
"Exactly the same."'

When Roy arrived in Hull on 9 November, 1949, the city was still recovering from World War Two. German bombers had pounded it throughout the conflict, reducing most of the city centre to rubble and leaving 85 per cent of homes damaged or destroyed. Well over a thousand people had been killed in bombing raids, and the deep scars left by the war could be seen well into the 1960s, when children still played in bomb sites from a generation before. The people of Hull felt their wartime suffering had not been recognised by the powers that be, a feeling which fed their long-standing sense of alienation from the rest of Britain.

Hull had never felt it was part of the mainstream of British life. In one of the key events which led to the English Civil War, it was the first town to defy King Charles I when it refused him entry in 1642. In 1911 the city was almost shut down by a wave of strikes, causing at least one shipowner to warn the government that a revolution could take place. By the 1950s, the centre of the city had been almost emptied of the middle classes, leaving it dominated by the culture of the industrial working-class. And at its heart was rugby league, a sport which itself was almost wholly proletarian. Like the city itself, the game prided on its inclusive, meritocratic traditions, but also on its difference. Its supporters liked to think they walked with their chests out and their heads high, because this was a sport which allowed working-class people to demonstrate their superiority over their so-called 'betters'.

Rugby had been entwined with Hull's self-identity for almost a century before Roy arrived there. Hull Football Club had been formed by the sons of the city's ship-owning and merchant families in 1865 when soccer and rugby were both still called 'football'. One of the oldest clubs of any type of football in Britain, it was the first Yorkshire side to join the RFU and soon established itself as one of northern rugby's powerhouses. Like all industrial cities in the north of England, Hull grew rapidly in the late 1800s and its population doubled to a quarter of a million by the end of the Victorian era. As the city grew, so too did rugby as thousands flocked to play and watch the game.

By the 1880s, Hull FC's ground was on Holderness Road, one of the arterial roads which sliced through the rapidly expanding eastern half of the city, the home of modern industrial areas and trading docks. Hull was split down the middle by the River Hull. The older, traditional heart of the city was based on the western side of the river. Here, daily life was dominated by trawler fishing in the fecund but icily-murderous waters of the far North Sea, an occupation which over a century and a half cost the lives of over 6000 Hull trawlermen.

It was in West Hull that thousands of trawlermen, dockers, and fish trades' workers lived among the tight-knit backstreets which branched off the long and unwinding Hessle Road as it ran parallel with the River Humber. On most days when trawlers were unloading their catches, a heavy and oppressive miasma of fish hung over Hessle Road. It was an unpleasant odour for visitors but a reassuring aroma for those whose livelihoods depended on the fruits of the sea. From this community emerged in 1882 what became the city's other professional rugby league team, Hull Kingston Rovers, formed by local shipbuilding apprentices. By the 1890s an east-west rivalry between Hull and Rovers, as the two teams would always be known by their supporters, deepened the local obsession with rugby.

And then something strange happened. In 1895, just at the point when rugby split into league and union, the two Hull clubs swapped locations. Hull, one of the founders of the new Northern Union, wanted a bigger ground than was available in East Hull. The city's largest stadium was the Boulevard, just off Hessle Road and at the heart of West Hull's fishing community. It also happened to be the home ground of Rovers. So Hull simply offered the Boulevard's owners more rent than Rovers could afford and moved across the city to take up residence there. In retaliation, Rovers moved across the River Hull to the east of the city. Opposition from fans was vocal but surprisingly short-lived. Within months of moving each club had become the symbol and the pride of their new side of the River Hull.

FROM CAPTAIN TO COACH

Roy ran out in Hull's famous black and white irregular-hooped shirt three days after he signed for the club. It was an away match at Keighley, and he was greeted by freezing, driving rain that was so heavy that the referee abandoned the match at half-time, just as Roy began to fear he was suffering from hypothermia. The rest of his season didn't get any better. He made his home debut against Halifax the following Saturday but damaged his knee ligaments. A cyst developed on the knee and in February 1950 he went into hospital for an operation to have it removed. When the season ended in April, Roy had played exactly one and a half matches for his new club.

Things were even worse for the team, which finished 19th out of the 29 sides in the league. It was its lowest position since 1931, and the season was capped off with a players' strike over bonus payments. On Good Friday, one of the city's two traditional rugby league derby days, Hull overcame Rovers 15-6 in front of 18,000 fans. As a semi-professional sport, rugby league players were paid on a win-loss basis. Hull players received £3 for winning a match and usually half that for a loss. Given the importance of the match and the size of the crowd, Hull captain Ernie Lawrence asked the club's directors if the players could have a bonus on top of their £3 winning money. The directors said no, and so the players refused to play in the final three games of the season.

Strikes were not uncommon in rugby league in the 1950s. Many players had day jobs in heavily unionised industries and were used to taking action in defence of their rights. Hull's dockers, many of whom were also rugby league players, were well-known for standing up for themselves. In 1954 they played a key role in creating a new militant dockers' union, the National Amalgamated and Stevedores Union, famously known as the 'Blue Union' for the colour of its membership cards. Hull FC's directors responded to the players' strike by telling them they would be replaced by reserve team players for the last few matches of the season. The strikers were less steadfast than they might have been in their daily jobs, and they eventually apologised to the directors. The apology was accepted but the directors then vindictively refused to pick any of the strikers for the final match of the season, which ended in a heavy defeat at Dewsbury.

Roy was still living in Wigan, recuperating from his knee operation, and wasn't involved in the strike. However, he was one of the major beneficiaries of its aftermath. The club's rowdy annual general meeting in July 1950 saw four new members elected to the nine-strong board of directors, together with a new chairman, Ernest Hardaker, the elder brother of future Football League secretary Alan Hardaker. The incoming board was keen to rebuild, and in August Roy was installed as the new club captain for the start of the new season.

With hindsight, Roy's appointment as captain marked the starting point for Hull's great 1950s team. His transfer in November 1949 was one of six key signings made by the club between 1949 and 1951. The sequence began with the recruitment of the tough teenage prop-forward Mick Scott from the local amateur club Boulevard Juniors in April 1949, followed by Roy, and then by Welsh rugby union hooker Tommy Harris in January 1950. Scott, Harris and Jim Drake, who signed from the amateur club Heworth in March 1951, would become the core of the club's powerhouse forward pack. Colin Hutton, a cultured goal-kicking full-back, moved across the country from Widnes in March 1951 to provide the team's sheet anchor.

Most importantly of all, in December 1950, the supremely fit, highly intelligent, all-round athlete Johnny Whiteley was signed from the local Hull Boys' Club team. Born a drop-kick away from the Boulevard stadium, Whiteley would eventually become Roy's heir, the club's greatest player, and its heart and soul for the next 70 years. As loose-forward, he led the forwards with his combination of relentless energy, ball distribution skills, and boundless enthusiasm for tackling. He was joined in the pack over the next 18 months by Harry Markham, Bob Coverdale and Jim Drake's twin brother Bill. They would soon constitute an almost unbeatable forward combination.

No one was surprised when the club named Roy as the new captain. Despite playing barely two hours of first-team rugby during the previous season, there wasn't a single doubting voice inside or outside of the club. So strong was the reputation that Roy had built as a leader of players during the 1940s that his accession to the captaincy was universally welcomed. Although no one drew the connection, it could also be viewed as a vindication of the outgoing board of directors, who had clearly signed him for his leadership qualities. Even so, it was Ernest Hardaker's new board which would garner the credit.

Not that there was much credit due from Roy's first season as captain. Although he was the team's top try-scorer with 12 touchdowns, Hull finished the season 18th in the league, just one place higher than the previous season. But behind the scenes, Roy had been extending his influence at the club. In February 1951 he was put in charge of the team's mid-week training, travelling from his Wigan home to the Boulevard to supervise training sessions.

Before this, the half dozen or so Hull players who lived in West Yorkshire or Lancashire did fitness training on their own and usually met only once during the week to prepare for Saturday's match. Looking beyond the current season, Roy told a reporter from the *Hull Daily Mail* that the players would start training in early July, to ensure the side's fitness and tactical awareness were at peak levels for the first match of the season at the end of August. As another reporter cryptically explained, Roy's ambition was 'to make headway in a direction that would keep him in the game when his playing days were over'.

His coaching ambitions were helped by the fact that Hull had not employed a coach since 1948. Although this may appear strange, the modern concept of the coach who takes complete charge of a team was not fully accepted until the 1960s. All rugby league teams had a trainer, but their job was just to get the players fit. Some trainers who had been star players – such as the former Wigan great Jim Sullivan who coached Wigan and St Helens in the 1950s or ex-Bradford player and long-time coach Dai Rees – were given responsibility for the tactical direction of the team, but at many clubs this was often the job of the captain and other senior players. Peter Harvey, who played representative rugby union before switching back to play for his hometown club St Helens, recalled that 'in the 1950s, training nights were twice a week for one hour each session. This included time to have a rub down and play "tick and pass" for the rest of the time. On special occasions the coaches might organise a cup of tea upstairs together with a social chat about next week's game'. The low priority attached to coaching could be seen in the fact that the Great Britain Lions touring side to Australasia did not appoint a coach until the 1958 tour.

Perhaps the strangest example of the unimportance attached to the coach's role was when Jim Sullivan left Wigan for St Helens in June 1952 and the club replaced him with a part-time masseur from Barrow. As in soccer, responsibility for selecting the team was always held by the board of directors. A coach might advise or suggest, but the ultimate choice was in the hands of the directors, a privilege to which they believed they were entitled by the money they had invested in a club. As one Hull director told Johnny Whiteley when he took over as Hull coach in 1963, 'You are a paid servant of this club.' Players, in directors' eyes, were their employees and the right to deal with them as they pleased was not something they would easily concede to a coach.

Hull previously had trainers who were seen as more than simply fitness advisers. In the late 1920s they appointed as coach Edgar Wrigley, one of the pioneering 1907 New Zealand rugby league tourists. As with Wrigley's other coaching appointments, this had not been successful. Former Hull stand-off Eddie Caswell replaced Wrigley and coached the team from 1931 to 1946, and was succeeded by another former player, the East Hull-born Ted Tattersfield. When Tattersfield resigned in June 1948 the board of directors didn't appoint a replacement coach. Eventually local physiotherapist Jack Murray, who according to the local newspaper was often 'called upon by the club when massage treatment has been required by players', was put in charge of fitness training. But building a ship without a rudder was unlikely to create the great team so sorely desired in West Hull.

Roy would have been very confident in his ability to take Hull to the top of the sport. He not only had the leadership skills, personal qualities and Army training to be a coach, he was also the senior, most experienced player on the club's books. Despite the poor season, Roy's standing at the club continued to grow. 'Roy Francis has done a wonderful job,' one shareholder told the club's annual general meeting in the summer of 1951. Based on watching Roy work with the players at training, the shareholder predicted that the 'prospects this season were bright'.

Under Roy's guidance Hull won its first five league matches of the 1951–52 season, and for the first time since the war the club found itself at the top of the league table. The club's directors now had no other choice. On 18 September, 1951 the *Hull Daily Mail* announced on its front page 'Roy Francis Hull Player-Coach', and reported the club had rewarded him with a two-year contract as the club's player-coach. It was a universally popular appointment. As the *Hull Daily Mail* hit the streets that warm September afternoon,

Roy and the family were driving through Hull with the car windows down. 'We stopped at some traffic lights and a bloke drove up alongside us and said, "Now then, Roy, how are you doing?" remembered Roy's son, Ian. "He was thrilled beyond measure to see my father."' The players were even more enthusiastic about the appointment than the supporters. 'The whole club erupted when Roy took over,' recalled Johnny Whiteley.

No sooner had Roy achieved his ambition of becoming a professional coach than he faced the biggest tragedy of his life. Little more than four weeks later, on 21 October, 1951, his mother Rebecca died after a stroke at her home in Brynmawr. She was 68 and had been suffering with heart problems for most of her later life. The whole family travelled down from Hull to see her, and as the last seconds of her life ebbed away she was surrounded by her extended family. 'She was in a coma and we were all sat round her,' remembered Ian Francis. 'The doctor told us that she could hear but she couldn't see. We were waiting for my dad, and when he came in the room, she turned her head and put her hand out to where he was – it was almost as if she could see. He came round the bed, sat down next to her and held her hand. And then she died.'

Whatever thoughts went through Roy's mind at that moment, he would have known that without her he would not have been the man he was. Rebecca had taken her husband's illegitimate son into her home, treated him as her own, and became both mother and father to him. She had brought him up, encouraged his talents, and taught him how to deal with prejudice. What he knew about being a man had not come from his absent father but from Rebecca. It was she who had equipped him with the tools to be successful, and gave him the confidence to step into the unknown and move to Wigan as a 17-year-old. This was a noble woman, whose kindness and sense of responsibility had rescued a little black boy and turned him into a leader of men. The fact they did not share the same blood was immaterial to her and her son. What counted was love, something which has always been thicker than blood or water.

'THE FRANCIS FORMULA'

Whatever the emotional impact of his mother's death, Roy did not let it interfere with his coaching responsibilities. Hull started winning regularly and the confidence of the side visibly grew. It was not only Roy's coaching abilities which were making the difference to the team. As he approached the late autumn of his playing career, he enjoyed one of his best seasons since the war. He stayed clear of serious injury and played in 35 of Hull's 42 matches, scoring 16 tries. 'One could also sense the inspiration which Francis was affording' to his teammates in their match against Huddersfield, wrote *Hull Daily Mail's* 'Kingstonian', the pseudonym of reporter Mike Ackroyd. On Boxing Day 1951, Hull beat a powerful Hunslet side 28-11 with the screw being turned when 'Francis intercepted, set off downfield at full speed, and timed his pass to Whiteley beautifully, so that the young loose-forward-cum-centre had no trouble in dashing the remaining 20 yards to score'. Roy even had the honour of scoring a last-minute try which sealed yet another derby win against Hull KR on Good Friday.

The derby win all but assured Hull a place in the top four of the league and qualification for the Championship play-offs. Rugby league in the 1950s had one division for all 30 professional sides, but not all sides played each other, so the league champions were decided by a top-four play-off system. The team finishing first played the fourth-placed side, while the second- and third-placed teams played each other. The winners then played each other in the Championship Final at a neutral venue. Hull finished in third place and so had to travel to a play-off match at second-placed Wigan.

The match was significant for many reasons. It was the first time in 16 years that Hull played in a championship play-off match, and it would also be the first time in eight years they had played Wigan, one of the dominant sides of the late 1940s. Roy would be returning to his first rugby league club, where his promising career had almost been derailed by Harry Sunderland. He was also pitting his coaching wits against his first rugby league coach, Jim Sullivan. 'Friendly, but hardly progressive' was how Roy would later remember his early mentor. For someone with Roy's innate self-confidence and love of the big stage, this was a game for which he was born.

It was also a moment for which Hull fans had been waiting. Thousands paid 12 shillings and sixpence to cram themselves onto special excursion trains to Wigan on the morning of the match. Despite heavy rain before kick-off and a pitch which had lost much of its grass, Hull repulsed wave after wave of Wigan attacks. Eventually the defence cracked when Wigan's New Zealand left winger Brian Nordgren – probably the only professional rugby league player who was also a qualified solicitor – scored a try next to the corner flag to put Wigan in the lead. But shortly before half-time, Hull scrum-half Don Burnell fed the ball to prop Mick Scott, who carried three Wigan tacklers over the line to score a try and make it 9-3 to Hull.

The intensity continued throughout the second half, but thanks to two more Nordgren tries, Wigan triumphed 13-9 in a pulsating match, and went on to win the Championship final. Hull fans' disappointment at the result was tempered by a realisation that, at last, a team coached by Roy Francis was more than capable of competing at the highest level.

Hull's success that season owed much to the fact they were considerably fitter than most of their opponents. Fitness was at the core of the Francis coaching philosophy. He began regular team training sessions in mid-July, almost two months before the season started, because it would give Hull 'the edge on everyone else for fitness, which would be vital to secure a winning start,' he explained. 'Confidence would grow and once a team gets a strong belief in themselves that's half the battle.' Their high fitness levels also ensured that his players could outlast their opponents and finish stronger at the end of matches.

His training techniques were derived from what he had learned during the war in the Army Physical Training Corps. 'His voice, demonstrations and patter were all in the dearly beloved service tradition,' reported Mike Ackroyd after observing Roy in a training session. In the gym, Roy used a wide variety of drills and exercises,

Roy Francis as a baby, photographed in Brynmawr *c.* 1921.

Wigan captain Jim Sullivan shows off the Lancashire Cup to new manager Harry Sunderland in October 1938 while the teenage Roy stands behind Sunderland.

Roy seated next to Eddie Waring, the manager of the all-conquering Dewsbury team in 1943, with rugby league's Championship and Challenge Cup trophies.

Roy and Bradford Northern's Ernest Ward eating oranges at half-time during the 1944 England versus Scotland international.

The England team at Gloucester's Kingsholm ground before the England v Wales Services' International rugby union match, 8th April, 1944. Roy scored a try in England's 20-8 win.

Maeers/Fox Photos/Hulton Archive

Trevor Foster, Ernest Ward (both Bradford Northern), Roy and Jimmy Stott (St Helens) during World War Two.

Simon Foster

Roy discusses tactics at half-time during Wales' 7-19 loss to France at Bordeaux in 1946.

Francis family

Roy making his Great Britain debut in 1947 against New Zealand, in which he scored two tries.

Francis family

Francis family

Roy shakes hands with the Earl of Derby before he plays for Warrington in the 1949 Rugby League Championship Final.

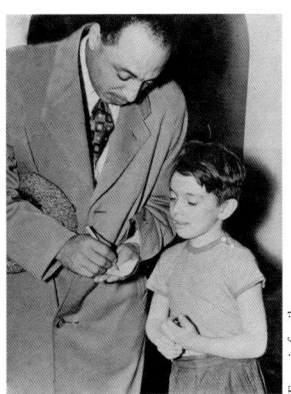

Francis family

Roy signs an autograph for a young Hull FC fan in the 1950s.

Francis family

A sharply dressed Roy leads a Hull training session at the club's Boulevard ground in 1952.

Roy leads the Hull team out at the Boulevard in the early 1950s.

Francis family

Roy in classic centre-threequarter action for Hull in 1953.

Francis family

Francis family

Hull return home with the Rugby League Championship trophy in 1956 and parade down Hessle Road, the heart of the city's fishing community.

Roy promotes Anglo-Australian trade links by eating Australian apples in front of Hull's Paragon Station in the late 1950s.

Rene, Geoff, Roy and Ian at home with the famous Bell & Howell Cine Camera in 1957.

Roy gives a pre-match talk at Wembley in 1959.

Rene Francis (centre) with nine wives of Hull players in 1959.

Ever the fatherly figure, Roy helps Johnny Whiteley with his scrum cap at Wembley in 1959.

Roy, cigarette in hand, watches the 1968 Challenge Cup Final from the Leeds bench at Wembley.

Roy, Jack Nelson, John Atkinson and Alan Smith before the 1968 Wembley Challenge Cup Final.

Roy and Rene arriving in Sydney on the SS *Canberra* in 1969.

Roy hosts a barbecue for North Sydney players and their wives in 1969.

Roy with his North Sydney Bears rugby league team in 1969.

John Raymond Elliott/Fairfax Media

Roy Francis addresses club members in the auditorium of the North Sydney Leagues Club in 1969.

Martin James Brannan/Fairfax Media

Roy explains tactics to North Sydney captain Ken Irvine during a training session in 1969.

Welsh prop forward Jim Mills playing snooker with Roy at North Sydney Leagues Club in 1970.

John M Manolato/Fairfax Media

Alyson Tippings

In 2023, 86 years after leaving his hometown, Roy is honoured with a statue in the centre of Brynmawr.

such as circuit training and physical jerks, as well as basketball for improving dexterity and hand-eye coordination. To improve players' sense of spatial awareness, he would get them to play soccer with two balls, forcing them to think about two situations at once. Roy also brought to training Tongan light-heavyweight boxing champion Sione 'Johnny' Halafihi, to whom he would later briefly become trainer, to show them sparring techniques to increase their fitness and stamina.

Players were also expected to take responsibility for keeping themselves fit outside of training sessions. By and large this was not difficult, as most players worked in manual jobs which required strength and fitness. Dockers were employed to lift and move heavy goods, bricklayers carried hods of bricks up and down ladders, and warehousemen spent their days shifting boxes. The young Johnny Whiteley worked on the fish docks: 'I was humping bloody great 10-stone kits of fish on and off a barrow, and then running a mile with them on my shoulders.' What we call weight training today was then part of workaday life for most of Hull's male workforce. Moreover, because many of Hull's players worked for employers who were at least sympathetic to the club, time could easily be found for extra training sessions during work-time. 'We became virtually full-time pro athletes,' recalled Johnny.

If improving players' strength was not a central feature of Roy's fitness regime, speed was at its very heart. Speed was the sting in the tail that would take Hull past their opponents during matches and across the entire season. Throughout his coaching career, sprint-training was the axis around which training revolved. One of the first things Roy did when he became Hull coach was to approach the local sports' outfitter, the alarmingly-titled 'Asbestos and Rubber Company', and ask them to supply their best sprinting shoes, known as spikes, to the club. Club folklore has it that a pipe-smoking director came in to look at the new equipment only to almost swallow his pipe when he saw the price labels attached to the spikes. But Roy insisted, and the players got their spikes because, as he later explained, 'In the professional game a pair of spikes in which to train is more important than football boots, for it is from them that you get your speed and balance.' When the players arrived in the dressing rooms a couple of days later to change for training, they were confronted with dozens of boxes of spikes. Roy asked them to choose a pair because from now on they would be wearing them at training. When he handed a pair to Tommy Harris, Hull's gifted Welsh hooker, Harris told him, 'I don't need them, Roy, I'm a hooker,' to which he received the reply, 'Yes, Tommy, and you're going to be a bloody fast hooker as well!'

To further improve their speed, Roy also built a 60-yards-long running track at the club's Boulevard ground so players could develop their sprinting technique. He and Johnny Whiteley marked out a track using the guidelines of the Amateur Athletics Association, flattened the surfaces, and then Roy persuaded the North Eastern Gas Board to deliver ashes so they could create a cinder running track. For longer runs to improve stamina training, Roy would take the players to Hull's athletic track at the nearby Costello Playing Fields. 'We were taught how to get from A to B with the least amount of exertion,' remembered Johnny.

This wasn't the first time that a rugby club had used sprinting as part of its training. In the 1920s, Huddersfield's trainer Albert Clayton used sprinting in spikes as part of fitness sessions, although according to the club's great prop-forward Douglas Clark, Clayton saw sprinting as a means to develop leg strength rather than speed. Roy saw sprinting as a means of increasing fitness, but it was also an end in itself. He not only wanted backs to move as quickly as possible, he also wanted his forwards, traditionally seen as slower and less athletic, to run like backs. It was this style of rugby that the journalist Jack McNamara would later call 'The Francis Formula'. 'Somewhere there are big men who can move like three quarters and I'm going to bloody well find them,' he told his son Ian. 'I'm looking for big guys that can run.' And to increase the team's competitive advantage, he also brought to training the sprint coach Harold Thrussell, one of only six professional sprint coaches employed by the Amateur Athletic Association.

Building a sprinting track and employing Thrussell were not Roy's only innovations. To improve his players' tackling technique, he hired a breakdown truck with a tow hook on the back, attached a tackle bag to it, and drove it up and down while the players took turns tackling the bag as it moved. During the hard winter months when the pitch was frozen, making it dangerous for players to dive or tackle, he arranged for the delivery of bales of hay to the ground. The hay was spread over the pitch so normal practice could take place without the risk of injury. It also helped strengthen the players legs. 'It was like trying to run in water,' remembered Roy's son Geoff, himself a talented teenage athlete who used to train with the team. To modern eyes, Hull's defensive system seems rudimentary – Roy's players simply 'numbered up', with each player facing their opposite number in a line and taking responsibility to tackle them, while Johnny Whiteley played in a sweeper role behind the defensive line to cover against any breaks. Even so, it proved highly successful, with Hull once going eight successive matches without conceding a try.

Roy's attacking tactics were similarly straightforward. By and large, the aim was to pass the ball until a gap was found in the opposing defence, which would then be exploited by the pace of the player who received the ball in the gap. 'I don't believe in stringing out for an obvious cross-field passing movement,' he explained before the 1956 Championship final. 'I tell my boys to line up in a sort of staggered formation so that when they receive the ball, they can go either way.' The fact that Roy trained his forwards to run and handle like backs – even though this was an era when matches sometimes produced 50 scrums and forwards prided themselves on their specialist scrummaging skills – meant that gaps were easier to find and chances more easily taken. The traditional big forward who left the running and passing to the backs had no place in Roy's teams. 'I train my forwards like backs. In fact, now and again in training, the backs pack down and the forwards line up,' he said in the same interview. This approach prefigured what might be called 'Total Rugby League' – in the spirit of Johan Cruyff's Dutch 'Total Football' of the 1970s – in which all players handled and ran like backs and tackled like forwards, coming to full fruition with the Australian Kangaroo touring teams of the 1980s.

Roy also developed a system of signalling to his players during a match. When he wanted the ball to be kept tight and in the middle of the field, he would put a white towel between his knees as a sign to the players on the pitch. When he wanted the ball to be played to the wingers, he would spread the towel across his knees as he opened his legs. The 'white towel signs' became so well known it is difficult to imagine that opposing teams didn't know about them, but knowing the signals and stopping the moves were two very different tasks. The towel was also occasionally used to tell Hull players that they could retaliate when provoked by the opposition. Roy always insisted that his players were well-disciplined and showed restraint when opponents tried to physically intimidate them. 'I want no fighting, no vendettas, just play football,' was his pre-match mantra. But when he waved the white towel in the air, he was telling his players that their opponents' intimidation had gone far enough and they could respond in kind.

Roy very firmly saw himself as an innovator. 'He was always looking for something different,' was how Johnny Whiteley summed up his attitude to coaching. He was rarely without his clipboard and pen to take copious notes about training and matches, and he also used a tape recorder to capture his thoughts. Most famously, he bought a Bell and Howell cine-camera to record training sessions and matches. At player meetings he would use the film to analyse where players positioned themselves during a match, and freeze-frame it at key points to explain where each player should have been standing. Although video analysis was used in American football in the 1950s, Roy was the first British coach in rugby or soccer to use film to analyse the game. The cine-camera showed just how far ahead of his fellow coaches he was. Despite the obvious benefits of filming matches, no one in British sport followed his lead until the 1980s. Although the technology was primitive – film had to be taken to a photographic studio to be developed and then edited by hand – its failure to catch on was also due to the generally low level of coaching expertise at the time. Playing experience and 'gut feeling' were valued more than expertise and scientific understanding.

Roy's ideas on coaching resembled more those of the pioneering football managers than coaches in either code of rugby. Indeed, in rugby union the very idea of coaching was anathema. The game's culture of amateurism expected players to organise themselves and decide their own tactics, which meant the RFU didn't even appoint its first England coach until 1969. In football, the manager evolved from the administrative role of club secretary, and reached its modern form in the person of Herbert Chapman, who took charge of all team matters on and off the field. He guided Huddersfield Town to the Football League Championship in 1924 and 1925, before moving to further glory with Arsenal in the 1930s. A small number of other football managers followed Chapman's template in the 1930s and 1940s. Frank Buckley was perhaps the most notable, managing Wolverhampton Wanderers from 1927 to 1944 (and spending two years at Hull City after the war). A veteran of World War One, he dominated his teams by fear but also insisted on high levels of fitness, promoted dancing as a way of improving balance, and claimed to use extract of monkey glands to enhance his players' performance. But unlike Roy, Chapman and Buckley also had responsibility for some of the business aspects of running a club. In fact, a 1965 survey of 76 football club managers found that all but three of them still had administrative and financial responsibilities on top of their team duties.

Unlike most of his soccer peers in the 1950s, Roy had total control over team selection from the start of his coaching career. Officially this was not the case, because he was required to submit a team-sheet for approval by the directors every Thursday night. But the directors invariably voted for their coach's choice. According to Johnny Whiteley, this was one of the most notable changes in the first few weeks of Roy's coaching regime. For the first time, the players knew why each one had been selected or not. It was the sheer force of Roy's personality which forced the board to agree to hand over its most valued privilege. A different board might take a different position, a fear he hinted at to the *Hull Daily Mail* shortly after being appointed coach: 'The biggest disadvantage the club has to work under is having to elect directors every twelve months. Our present board have a policy which has succeeded. If you break that up next season I think it would be fatal.'

As his power over the board demonstrated, the single most important factor in Roy Francis' coaching methods was Roy Francis himself. Like his father, Roy was a highly intelligent and hugely charismatic figure, whom others looked towards as a natural leader. Johnny Whiteley, whose father had spent long years away from home working at sea, remembered him 'as such a man of the world, he was unique. We players looked up to him as a father figure'. Roy was not afraid of sometimes being a stern father to his players either. When the young Hull fan Keith Pollard – who himself would become a professional player in the 1960s – was waiting outside of the Boulevard for players' autographs in the mid-1950s, he was ignored by Hull prop-forward Bill Drake as he rushed to training. But Roy saw what had happened and sent Drake back to sign Keith's autograph book. 'He's been waiting a long time for you, Bill,' Roy admonished Drake.

Roy's attitude to young fans was part of the family atmosphere which he and Rene worked hard to create among the players and their wives. They took great pains to involve wives and girlfriends in the team's off-field activities and foster a spirit of camaraderie throughout the club. 'Happy wife, happy life' was the phrase that was often used by the couple to emphasise the relationship between harmonious family relationships and success on the field. As well as organising trips to matches, Rene would arrange social outings for wives, and often act as an adviser and confidante to them in much the same way as Roy did to his male players.

Although they both enjoyed their role of being *in loco parentis* to the young men and women who were part of the club, their ultimate goal was to create a better team by creating an environment in which players had the unquestioning support of the wives. As Roy explained, 'When a footballer finishes training, he brings his worries, fears, injuries, disconsolation and happiness home to his wife. She should realise that football is his first love.' In other words, a 'happy wife' had to accept her position; this was not a policy to empower women, but even so, the emphasis on building a family atmosphere at the club contrasted sharply with the traditional ideas about team-building which were prevalent in sport at that time.

Many soccer managers and rugby league coaches felt that wives and girlfriends were a distraction for their players and tried to impose a rigorous separation between the sexes. Roy and Rene brought them together, sometimes literally. Johnny Whiteley was introduced to his future wife Joan by Roy and a number of players met their wives at one of the pubs Roy ran or at his cafe, the Haversnack, in nearby Beverley. Tongan centre three-quarter Nan Halafihi met his wife at the cafe, and it was also where Geoff Francis met his wife Anne. The family ethos extended to providing players with lodgings. Frankie Broadhurst, the stand-off half who signed from Halifax in 1957, was one of many players who actually lived in the Francis family home when they came to Hull, so much so that Roy's son Geoff said he was almost like another brother in the family. Clive Sullivan and his brother Brian also lived at the Francis house when the two of them moved from Cardiff to play for Hull.

More than any other British sports coach in the 1950s, Roy focused on the whole player, on and off the field. The qualities that he valued in a player were those he valued in himself, an attitude he articulated later during an interview on Australian television when he was asked, 'What are the basic things a coach requires?' He replied by stating, 'Knowledge, dedication, honesty and sincerity.' When he was then asked what he required from players, he shot back, 'Exactly the same.' Although other coaches used innovative training methods, learned from other sports, and sought to develop the character of their players, only Roy had mastery of coaching techniques, absolute loyalty from his players, and complete deference from his board of directors. All he had to do was to deliver success to his club.

LONG ROAD TO GLORY

This was not so easily achieved. After the near-glory of reaching the championship semi-final in Roy's first season as coach, the next three seasons were something of an anti-climax. In the 1952–53 season, the club slumped to finish 15th in the league. Roy played in over half of Hull's matches, but he was struggling to stay fit. In September 1952 he was hospitalised with appendicitis and then tore a stomach muscle in the Boxing Day match with Hunslet, both of which meant weeks of convalescence. He was now aged 33, and retirement was beckoning. When he was asked at a sports forum in October 1952 if the rugby league season was too long he replied, 'At my age the season is too long – and so is the pitch!'

As part of his post-playing retirement planning, in December 1952 Roy took over the management of the Hawthorn Hotel, a large three-storey pub built in 1875 that was just a mile away from Hull's Boulevard ground. When he first signed for the club, Roy commuted between his home in Wigan and Hull, but when he was made the team coach, he moved to the city and spent his first summer living at the White Horse Hotel, a prominent pub in the city centre. The family then moved into a large house at 620 Beverley Road, the main arterial route north out of the city. Those were days when one of the perks of being a high-profile rugby or football player was to become a pub landlord, and it is probable that during the negotiations which led to him becoming the coach, Hull told Roy they would set him up with a pub to manage. As the *Hull Daily Mail* pointed out, there were six other sportsmen already running pubs in the city, who would shortly be joined by Hull players Colin Hutton and Mick Scott. Like all industrial cities, the links between Hull's drinks trade and its sports teams ran deep, and Roy running a pub continued a long tradition which stretched back to the 1890s, when Hull Brewery sponsored the local rugby annual handbook.

Roy had hoped that managing the Hawthorn would be a business which would set him up for a stable post-playing career. But the pub was not lucrative and Roy suspected that the brewery was using his name just to shore up a failing business. Within a couple of years he moved on and became the landlord of the Lambwath, a large modern pub in east Hull. This time the pub was successful, but the brewery's area manager constantly complained that it was underperforming and asked Roy to pay amounts up to £100 every few months to cover what he claimed was a shortfall in takings. In the end, Roy decided that he could not afford it anymore and the family reluctantly left the pub and moved out of the living accommodation above it. Roy and Rene had no doubt about the reason for the loss of the Lambwath. 'That's what the area manager wanted,' recalled Ian Francis. 'He wanted my dad out because he didn't like coloured people.' A few weeks later, the new licensee of the pub was named as a local retiring police superintendent.

The family's forced move out of the Lambwath left them homeless, and they had to split up temporarily until Roy found a new home. 'He and my mum went to live with Tommy Harris, and me and my brother Geoff went to stay with Colin Hutton,' explained Ian Francis. It was a painful move and left Roy traumatised. As an illegitimate mixed-race child, he had been saved from the orphanage by Rebecca Francis, who had instilled in him a fervent love of a secure family life, but now he felt he had not been able to protect his own family. 'When we got out of the car to go to Colin's,' said Ian, 'I turned back and I could see he was crying. My mother said he was broken-hearted because his family had been split up through no fault of his own.'

Roy never confided these humiliations with any members of his team, and maintained the outward appearance of the totally committed coach. In the 1953–54 season, Hull finished fifth in the league and reached the final of the Yorkshire Cup before going down 7-2 to Bradford Northern. But time was now running out for Roy's playing career. He was injured twice in the first two months of the season, and then again in a Boxing Day match against Hunslet when he also scored four tries for the first time in his career. The following season he managed just 11 matches, before deciding in October 1954 that the downward spiral of recurring injuries was the signal to announce his retirement from playing. However, a string of poor results led him to rescind his retirement decision and he returned to play in early December. But it was to no avail and Hull finished 19th in the league, their lowest position for five years.

Roy had now been Hull's coach for four years and pressure was mounting on him to deliver silverware. The 1955–56 season began as a copy of the previous one. Hull played 16 matches in the first 10 weeks, once again ending up with a Yorkshire Cup final against Halifax. This time the tables were almost turned in a thrilling but brutal drawn match. Fighting broke out in the scrum several times, and Halifax's John Henderson was sent off for injuring Johnny Whiteley. Such was the ire of the Hull fans that Henderson was accompanied by a police escort as he walked to the dressing rooms. The disappointment of being so close yet so far was magnified even further when Hull lost the replay 7-0.

Perhaps it was the belief that they should have, and could have, beaten Halifax that sent a bolt of confidence surging through the team. Over the course of the next six months, Hull lost just six league matches, and finished the season fourth in the table, qualifying for the Championship semi-finals. Finishing fourth earned them an away tie against Roy's old club, Warrington, the team which had finished top of the league. They had won the championship the previous season and done the league and cup double the year before that. What's more, the Wire had not suffered a home defeat by a Yorkshire side for 18 years.

Hull's inexperienced team was given little chance, yet they overran and outplayed Warrington's champion team to win by an astounding 17-0. It was a tactical triumph for Roy, who had planned for his forwards to neutralise the Warrington pack by rushing up quickly to suffocate them in the tackle and, in attack, using his lighter forwards' speed and handling skills to tire their opponents. Two tries at the end of the match were a testament to his philosophy of fitness that lasted to the very last second. Hull would now appear in their first major final since 1935.

Their opponents were Halifax, their adversaries in the epic Yorkshire Cup Final earlier that season. Now Hull had to go one better and defeat the West Yorkshire team in a final. Like Warrington, Halifax were also one of the game's dominant sides, beaten finalists in two of the last three championship finals and the narrow losers of the 1954 and 1956 Challenge Cup finals. They had built their success on their heavy, aggressive pack of forwards who, as Hull had found during the Yorkshire Cup Final earlier in season, sought to subdue their opponents through strength and intimidation. But the earlier final had shown that the greater speed and mobility of the Hull forwards could undermine the physicality of Halifax. This was a match-up that Roy relished, pitting his Total Rugby philosophy up against a powerful yet more traditional side.

In preparation, he took the team to stay in Blackpool on the Friday and travelled to the final venue, Manchester City's Maine Road ground, on the Saturday morning. They had a light training session before boarding the coach to take them to Manchester for the club's biggest day in two generations. Back home in Hull, thousands of fans boarded seven special excursion trains which left the city's Paragon Station every 10 minutes from 9 a.m. Others boarded countless coaches that had been hired for the day – some from as far away as Nottingham, due to the clamour to see the final – while thousands of others made the journey in private cars, the first time that significant numbers of cars had travelled from Hull to a cup final.

As the 37,000 crowd gathered in anticipation, Roy gave his teamtalk in the dressing room. His plan was to keep the ball tight in the forwards in the early stages of the first half, causing Halifax to bunch their forwards in the middle of the pitch. Then, once Halifax had settled down to a forward battle, he would spread his white towel across his knees to signal to the players that they should spread the ball wide and use the full width of the pitch to attack down their opponent's wings. As usual, Roy wanted the players to make a fast start and establish a lead in the first half, knowing that their superior fitness would ensure they would not fade in the second half.

The Maine Road pitch was hard and dry, and the long soccer season had removed much of the grass from the surface. Hull faced a strong wind in the first half, something which favoured the tactical kicking game of Halifax's international loose forward, Ken Traill. Hull played exactly as instructed by Roy, and on 30 minutes they made the breakthrough when Bob Coverdale broke through a

tackle, offloaded the ball to Whiteley, who whipped it back inside
to a charging Tommy Harris, who touched down under the posts.
Full-back Colin Hutton kicked the conversion and Hull led 5-0.
Everything was going to plan until right-winger Brian Darlington
had to leave the field after injuring his knee in a crunching tackle
by his opposite number, Halifax's great black Welsh winger Johnny
Freeman. Down to 12 players – substitutes weren't allowed until
1964 – Hull maintained their lead until referee Charlie Appleton
blew for half-time.

Darlington came back for the second half, but immediately
revealed how bad his injury was when he couldn't get into position
for the kick-off and dropped the ball. But as Halifax were sensing
blood, Hull scrum-half Tommy Finn intercepted a pass from their
winger Arthur Daniels and touched down in the corner to make
it 8-0. But Halifax were still not beaten and sought to exploit the
injured Darlington on Hull's right. Two minutes after the Finn
try, they were back in it with an unconverted Geoff Palmer try.
Halifax forced Hull onto the back foot as they tried to exploit
the hobbling Darlington. Playing with only 12 fit players, Hull
seemed tired and listless as they tried to repel wave after wave of
blue and white shirts. On the hour, Arthur Daniels scored in the
right-hand corner to narrow Hull's lead to 8-6. And then, with just
eight minutes remaining, Hull's fabled fitness seemed to fail them
as a magnificent Ken Traill pass found Johnny Freeman, who swept
by the Hull defence to score in the left corner. Halifax now led 9-8,
and it seemed Hull would once again be frustrated in a final.

As the clock ticked down, the last reserves of energy built up
by Roy's fitness regime trickled back into the Hull players. With
less than three minutes to go, they were 30 yards from the Halifax
try line when referee Charlie Appleton awarded Hull a penalty
close to the left touchline. They had the option of tapping the ball
and trying to score a try or opting to kick a penalty goal for the
match-winning two points. It was not an easy choice for captain
Mick Scott. Kicker Colin Hutton had already missed with three
of his four shots at goal. And this was the most difficult kick of
them all. Scott looked over to the bench on the opposite touchline

where Roy was sitting. 'Take the kick, take the kick!' Geoff Francis remembers his father shouting animatedly from the sideline. Scott had no choice but to hand the ball to Colin Hutton.

Hutton had never hit a ball so surely and sweetly. It sailed over the Halifax crossbar and between the posts to make it 10-9 to Hull with seconds remaining. There was barely time to restart the match before Appleton blew the whistle, and thousands of Hull fans poured onto the pitch to raise Hutton up on their shoulders, followed by Scott, who held the Championship trophy aloft as the crowd carried him around Maine Road in a spontaneous lap of honour. At long last, Hull were the champions of rugby league – and no one doubted that the credit belonged to Roy Francis.

6

Triumph and Torment:
1956–1963

'The other was me.'

At the end of May 1956 Roy Francis bestrode the world of rugby league. He had been an outstanding player, but now he was also the most innovative coach in the sport, and on his way to becoming an icon of the city of Hull. Few men inspired such loyalty and devotion from those they led.

Yet there was one very obvious fact about him that was almost never mentioned. His skin colour.

Unlike most of his time in Wigan, Roy was not the only black person in Hull. As a port, it was home to a small black community which had lived there since the turn of the century. In 1920 the *Hull Daily Mail* estimated there were between 60 and 100 'coloured seamen now resident' in the city. In contrast to Liverpool or Bristol, Hull had few links with the slave trade. Slave traders and plantation owners had bought property in the East Riding countryside outside Hull, but the city's wealth had been built on trade with northern Europe and deep-sea fishing in the North Sea. Its major connection with slavery was William Wilberforce, the otherwise conservative MP who led the move to ban the trading of enslaved people in 1807, who was born there.

One of the seamen who made his home in Hull was a Sierra Leonean, Adolphus Meheux, who settled in Harrow Street, one of the densely packed streets in the fish docks area of Hessle Road. In 1901 he married Agnes Mawson and had five children, but their life together ended in May 1917 when his ship was sunk by German destroyers, leaving him and 10 crew-mates dead. Four months after he died, his eldest son Ralph made a try-scoring debut for Hull against Hull KR. This was the first of 13 games Ralph played for Hull during the war before being transferred to York in 1919. He never played in York's first team and soon returned to Hull to play amateur rugby league.

Hull's local black community largely escaped the terrifying riots that swept through Cardiff, Liverpool, Glasgow and many other port cities in 1919, but the severe rise in unemployment and the 'divide and rule' wage differentials of the shipowners meant Hull was not free of open racism. Sporadic violence was an occupational hazard for non-white seamen, and on the weekend of 19 and 20 June, 1920, a racist riot broke out which caused numerous injuries and led to the arrest of four black sailors. No white rioters were arrested despite the fact that the homes of at least five black families were attacked.

The violence quickly subsided, but many black seamen moved out of Hull as the industry recovered from the post-war depression. The Meheux family stayed in Hull, where their descendants still live today. Others also remained, such as the families of rugby league player Keith Barnwell, boxer Sammy Reed, and Leon Riley, a singer who started his working life as a docker and is remembered as the man who compered the first Beatles' concert in Hull in 1962. Future league player Bakary Diabira was born in the city in 1949 to a white mother and a Mauritanian father. By the time that Roy arrived the city liked to believe it was free of what was called 'race prejudice' and the memory of the racist riot of 1920 had been largely forgotten by its white population.

It is unlikely that Roy knew anything about Hull's ugly events of 1920, despite his childhood being shaped by the collective memory of the 1919 racist riots in South Wales. In the family environment he built around his team, he never gave any indication to players that racism had affected him. He even told the *Yorkshire Post* reporter Raymond Fletcher that he thought his skin colour made him stand out more in the sport and helped to raise his profile. Yet this public statement masked a much more complex reality. To some who knew him well, there were small clues which indicated he was always conscious of racism in everyday life. Johnny Whiteley remembered that Roy would always avoid going into pubs on his own. If someone suggested to him that they should meet in a pub, Roy would always suggest an alternative. The reason was simple. He knew that the volatile mix of alcohol and macho braggadocio significantly increased the chances of him being subjected to racist insults or even assault.

This wariness was part of the everyday armour that black people had to wear when they were out and about. Clive Sullivan took a similar approach. Ian Francis remembered going to a party with him in Hull in the 1960s. 'We were stood outside waiting around and I said to Clive, "Come on now, let's get stuck in," but he was the only black guy there and he said, "It's all right for you," and I said, "What do you mean?" And he said, "Well, look at me," so we had a couple of drinks and left.' Charlie Williams, who grew up as the only black person in his Yorkshire pit village before finding fame first as a footballer and then as a comedian, described how 'if I went into a pub, or into a room, I could sense if there was likely to be trouble. I could feel it in the air. And before I'd court trouble, I'd move off. I've never wanted it, whether I've been in the right or not.' Roy didn't even take the risk of testing the atmosphere. Racism 'is rather like flu,' he told Australian journalist Mike Gibson. 'You know you've got it but you don't quite know where it is.' So he simply refused to put himself in situations that he could not control.

Sometimes he had no choice but to confront racists. One evening late in 1954, when the family were living on the outskirts of Hull in a village called Cottingham, Geoff and Ian Francis returned home to find their parents visibly upset. 'When we walked in, we knew something had gone on,' said Ian. 'My mother was crying, and I said, "What's up?" My dad didn't want to talk about it but my mother did. Apparently they'd been out – and a black man with a white woman was still seen as a problem for some people back then – and some youths had started calling my mother names, so my dad had set about them.'

At school, Ian would fight other boys who used racist insults about him or his father. He gave up after Roy had been the guest of honour at his school's prize-giving day and unknowingly spoke to one of Ian's tormentors. The next day the bully told Ian that he was amazed his father was 'just like us'. After that, recalled Ian, 'I gave up fighting because I thought what's the point?'

Roy told his sons that 'you can't fight prejudice' and, unless physically threatened, simply refused to engage with racist behaviour. One night during the early 1950s the family was travelling back to Hull from Wigan on a foggy evening. In the days before motorways, this was a long and potentially hazardous journey in winter, so Roy stopped at a hotel in Halifax. Rene and the boys went to the reception desk while he parked the car. 'My dad came in and joined us,' recounted Ian. 'The desk clerk then said, "Is he with you?" so my mother replied, "Yes, this is my husband." The desk clerk said, "I'm sorry but we're completely full." My dad said, "OK" and we just walked out.' Roy refused to endure humiliation or give racists the satisfaction of knowing they had hurt him.

Rene shared her husband's refusal to engage with racists. As a white woman married to a black man in the 1930s, she would have been acutely aware of racist insults, whether deliberately expressed towards her or said unknowingly by those who didn't realise she was in a mixed marriage. In the early 1960s, when Roy was the coach at Leeds, Rene went to measure up for curtains in a house they wanted to buy in north-east Leeds. As she was getting her tape measure, the owner of the house asked if she was related to Roy Francis, the rugby league coach. Rene assumed she was a fan and said, 'Yes, he's my husband' only for the house-owner to reply, 'I'm awfully sorry but we've decided not to sell you the house.' Rene simply picked up her things and left.

For Roy, 'Racialism, discrimination, whatever you like to call it, is so very difficult to tabulate ... so very difficult. You see it as subtle differences in the feeling of someone towards you, subtle changes, remarks, acceptance one moment, non-acceptance the next.' This ever-present shadow of discrimination or humiliation was something that no black person or their partner could ignore. It could appear at any time and in different forms.

Roy had the advantage of being a coach of a rugby league club, an environment over which he had total control. His insistence on complete authority over the team was interpreted by the press as a characteristic of a master coach, but this control also reduced the chances that he would have to encounter racism. No player would ever make a racist remark in front of Roy, and anyone who considered doing so knew their teammates would see it as a betrayal of the team. When Hull signed the white South African rugby union player Mervyn 'Pin' McMillan in October 1957, Roy drove over to Manchester to pick him up from the airport. Coming from apartheid South Africa, McMillan probably could not conceive that his new boss would be black. As they made their way to Roy's car, McMillan told him, 'In my country you would be carrying my bags for me.' According to Ian Francis, Roy simply replied, 'No, we don't do that in this country' and drove to Hull in silence. McMillan never played for Hull's first team.

Roy's total authority within the club created what today would be called a safe space for himself and other black players. This made his teams unique in British sport at that time. The danger of 'everyday' racism from teammates – often dismissed as 'banter' – was a constant worry for black players. Leeds winger Alan Smith remembers discussing the problem with his Great Britain captain, Clive Sullivan. 'You can call me what you want, supporters do,' Clive told him. 'But I just don't like that word n----r.' Cec Thompson also recalled the pain he felt when his Workington Town teammate, Australian centre Tony Paskins, called him an Uncle Tom. Fifty years later, Thompson was still raw from the hurtful insult.

Although they were outwardly very sociable, Roy and Rene rarely had visitors to their home. 'They didn't like people calling round the house,' recalled Ian. 'We didn't have friends calling in for a cup of tea.' This gatekeeping by the couple ruled out any possibility that overt or 'casual' racism could be expressed in their family home. Their only visitors were players who were in need of advice or a helping hand. Johnny Whiteley lodged with the Francises after he left home in the early 1950s, as did Frankie Broadhurst, who stayed with them for over 18 months after he was signed from Halifax in 1957.

In 1960, Hull signed the young Tongan centre Nanumi 'Nan' Halafihi, who spent the first few months of his time in Hull staying with the Francis family above their Haversnack cafe in Beverley, the market town just north of Hull. Nan came to England with his brother, boxer Sione 'Johnny' Halafihi, who won the British Empire Light Heavyweight title in 1958. The following year, Clive Sullivan, like Roy born in South Wales, also stayed with Roy and Rene at the start of a rugby league career which would culminate in him captaining Great Britain to victory in the 1972 Rugby League World Cup.

Clive and Nan were the two most prominent names of the four black players who played for Hull during Roy's tenure as coach. Keith Barnwell joined in 1961 from a local youth club side and Clive's brother Brian signed in March 1962. Neither had the success of Clive – few players did – but were first team regulars for three or four seasons in the early 1960s. Nan Halafihi's career at Hull lasted barely a year, but he did have the honour of playing at Wembley in the 1960 Rugby League Challenge Cup final.

Nan's son, the rugby league player and university lecturer Dr Nick Halafihi, remembered how, 'My dad was always having to experience real difficulties because of his colour on and off the field,' and that, 'All through the sixties, he had a tough time with his colour, which may have reflected some of the experiences Roy may have had.' There were occasions when the racial abuse from an opposing player was so bad that Nan would say to them, 'I'll see you behind the stand to sort the difference out' after the match. Like Roy, Nan sought to protect those around him from the awful reality of racism and never told his family about it. It was only after

Nan died that Hull hooker Tommy Harris told Nick about the abuse his father had suffered.

Although Roy never spoke about abuse he received from fans and opposing players, he certainly experienced it. In 1964 Cyril Briggs, the editor of the weekly *Rugby Leaguer*, stated, 'Roy Francis had every reason to complain to me about certain attitudes.' Roy may have complained to certain journalists, but the one thing he did not do was to complain about racism while on the pitch. Rugby league's masculine culture was based on the principle of never letting your opponent see weakness. 'Never let them know you're hurt' was drummed into players from the day they picked up a ball, and this attitude meant that racism was rarely confronted by black players on the field.

Clive Sullivan's attitude to dealing with racism was similar to Roy's. 'It's done me a favour, because I stood out,' he told his wife Ros about his skin colour. She remembered that his attitude to racial abuse, 'Wasn't confrontational. He'd think, "Yeah. Well, I'll show you what I can do."' Ray Atkinson, a young black rugby player from Hull, was coached in the 1980s by Clive, who told him to ignore racist taunts: '"They are trying to get under your skin," [Sullivan] said. "Turn round and smile. The best way to silence them is by scoring tries."' This attitude of 'turning the other cheek' to racism would serve black players well, until they were faced with more overt and unavoidable racism.

Unlike his father, Roy was not a political man. 'There was never any talk about what the government was doing. He wasn't interested in politics at all,' explained his son Geoff. Racism for Roy was an individual question, something to be avoided or overcome, not something he wanted to campaign against. He tried to break down racial barriers through his personal actions. Just as he created an inclusive environment at his rugby clubs, he did the same in his two businesses in Beverley. His pub, the Cross Keys, and the nearby Haversnack cafe were places where black people could safely mix with local white people. Johnny Freeman and Colin Dixon, two black Welsh-born rugby league players, came to stay there for a break when they were playing for Halifax. In 1956, Roy was granted a licence to have live music in the Cross Keys at weekends, which he said would provide 'entertainment of a new style with an electric organ and drums'. Hull singer Leon Riley would appear there and Roy sometimes duetted with him or played the drums. Roy also installed an American jukebox in the pub, which he claimed was the first jukebox in east Yorkshire.

Over the road, the Haversnack cafe became the trendiest place in the town, attracting teenagers and young people as the rock and roll revolution began in the late 1950s. The cafe was also known as somewhere for black and white to mix freely, not a small thing in a society where racial mixing between the sexes could still be a matter for the police. In May 1959, a 16-year-old white girl in Hull was sent to a remand home because she refused to obey her parents and stop socialising with men from the city's small Arab community. Roy's cafe provided space for music and dancing for everyone, and its success could be measured by the fact that the Haversnack was where both Nan Halafihi and Roy's son Geoff met local girls whom they later married.

Roy's ability to shield himself and others from everyday racism was entirely unspoken. He almost never made public comments about race. There was just one exception, when he perhaps unwittingly revealed the full importance of the issue to him. In March 1962 Hull signed Clive Sullivan's brother Brian, which caused Roy to ask in his *Hull Daily Mail* column: 'If Brian gets a run in the first team along with his brother will it be the first time a club side have had two coloured players holding down the wing positions? The answer is "'No'". Way back in the 1930s Barrow played two coloured lads on opposite wings in the first team for some considerable time. One was a lad who had the wonderful name of Valentine Cumberbatch, and the other was me.'

Whereas Lionel Francis sought to defy racism through political action, Roy sought to shield himself and others from it by using his personal success to create an extended surrogate family. And from his vantage point in the 1950s, he believed he had been successful. Not only was he a famous rugby coach, but he was also the only black coach in British professional sport. More significantly, he was quite probably the only black person to be a leader of white people in any walk of life anywhere in Britain. This was not only a significant achievement, but it was also a heavy burden.

SUCCESS BREEDS SUCCESS

Roy realised that this unique position was, to some extent, due to the fact that he led a winning team. A losing team would open the door to recriminations and insults, and the shield Roy had built to safeguard himself and his family would start to crack. So he was doubly motivated to make sure that Hull's championship triumph in 1956 would not be its last.

His first major decision in the quest to retain the championship was perhaps the most ruthless. He removed the captaincy from Mick Scott, the man who led Hull's triumph at Maine Road. Scott grew up close to the Boulevard stadium, joined the club as a teenager, and was made club captain in his early twenties. But as loved as he was by supporters, Roy felt that Scott was not mentally strong enough to be captain. When Scott's father died suddenly, he was bereft. 'Mick lost a bit of his appetite for the game when his dad died,' recalled Johnny Whiteley. 'He was never the same again.' For Roy, the captain was his representative on the pitch and he demanded complete commitment to his cause. Whiteley, with whom Roy was already conferring about tactics before matches, was handed the captaincy. It was the fulfilment of Johnny's childhood dream, but it was also an example of the ruthlessness with which Roy could operate.

He displayed the same hardness when the team did not follow his game plan in a match that Hull won easily at Castleford. As the players were congratulating themselves, chairman Ernie Hardaker went into the dressing room to congratulate the team and tell them they would get an extra bonus on top of their usual winning money. To everyone's surprise, Roy turned on his players, telling Hardaker that, 'I wouldn't have given them anything. I wouldn't give them a penny.' Johnny Whiteley remembered that Roy's outburst stunned everyone into silence, and he then refused to speak to the players on the coach back home to Hull. The silence continued throughout the following week and beyond the next match until Whiteley tried to mediate. 'I went and sat next to him,' he said. 'But by the time I'd finished, I had to apologise to him. When I came away, I thought, bloody hell, that's typical. But he was alright after that.' Roy knew there was more than one way to get what he wanted.

But most of the time his family-based approach got the desired results. That was certainly his strategy in the quest to retain the championship when the 1956–57 season began. With the exception of replacing Scott with Whiteley as captain, Roy essentially made no changes to the team's line-up, and that stability paid dividends. The club's league form was even more impressive than in the previous season, winning four more games and finishing the season second in the league table. In the championship semi-final they demolished a Barrow team which was in the running to complete a league and cup double. That win earned Hull a week off before facing Oldham in the Championship Final. Oldham was to cotton what Hull was to fishing. It was once home to Britain's largest textile factory, one of 350 cotton mills that dominated the skyline of 'Spindledom' in the interwar years, and the town's self-confidence was reflected in its high-spending rugby club that played with flair and swagger.

Just as in 1956, the 1957 Championship Final went down to the very last seconds of the match. After 45 minutes Hull led 11-5, but then Hull prop Cyril Sykes was injured in a tackle. As he tried to stand up to play the ball, he dropped the ball. The referee penalised him and Oldham's metronomic kicker Bernard Ganley kicked the goal. As so often happens in tight matches the momentum swung back to Oldham. With five minutes left, they led 15-11. Then, out of the blue, Hull's Scottish winger Ron Cowan pounced on an Oldham mistake and raced downfield to score a try to make it 15-14. A successful conversion would make it 16-15 to Hull. Once again, the fate of the Championship rested with the boot of Colin Hutton. He had kicked all his previous attempts at goal and if he converted Cowan's try, Hull would retain their title. But he edged his kick wide and, despite a frenzied Hull attack in the remaining few seconds, Oldham took Hull's crown.

In response to this agonising defeat, Roy set about refreshing the team. Full-back Colin Hutton retired and crossed the city to coach Hull KR, the first graduate of the Roy Francis school of coaching. The young Frankie Broadhurst was bought from Halifax to replace Roly Moat at stand-off. The experiment in signing the South African three-quarter Pin McMillan was scuppered after he insulted Roy at Manchester airport, so the club focused on local rather than overseas players to renew the side.

There was almost one stunning departure from this 'home-grown' policy. In December 1957 Hull approached Wigan about signing Billy Boston. Ever since he joined Wigan as a 19-year-old in March 1953, Boston had been a superstar. He scored 12 tries in his first five matches for the club, and after his sixth game was selected for the 1954 Lions tour to Australia and New Zealand. Built like a Sherman tank and possessing the grace of Rudolf Nureyev, Boston became the youngest player – and the first black player – ever to tour Down Under. The sheer brilliance of Boston dazzled all who saw him.

As his Wigan career accelerated, he nonchalantly broke all of the club's try scoring records and soon became universally loved by its fans. But the club was still run on the paternalist principles of the Victorian factory. In 1956 the directors humiliated Billy when they made him write an apology for his performance during the club's narrow loss in a Challenge Cup semi-final. Playing with an ankle injury in the unfamiliar position of centre three-quarter, he was accused of arriving late in the dressing room before kick-off. In fact, he had been looking for his pregnant wife Joan to make sure she had a ticket for a seat. It's difficult not to draw the conclusion that the directors needed a scapegoat, and the stereotype of the lazy, undisciplined black man made it easy for them to blame Billy.

The love felt for Boston across rugby league did not necessarily protect him from racism. In 1957 RFL secretary Bill Fallowfield concocted an injury story to leave Billy out of a short tour of apartheid South Africa on the way home from the Rugby League World Cup in Australia. The weekly *Rugby League Gazette* protested that in rugby league, 'We have no colour bar, we judge a man as a man irrespective of colour and everyone good enough is eligible to play for the country of their birth. That is as it should be and anyone who tinkers with this in order to "fit in" with South African standards is dealing a death blow at every civilised concept of sportsmanship.'

In August 1964, Billy responded to racist insults from a spectator at Swinton by going into the grandstand to find the perpetrator, who decided that discretion was the better part of cowardice and ran off.

But Billy was too big a star for Wigan to lose, and Roy's attempts to lure him to East Yorkshire came to nothing. So Hull began the 1957–58 season with a team which was probably of middling quality at best, with only Johnny Whiteley and Tommy Harris being regular international players. Even so, the campaign began with a spectacular nine-try rout of Challenge Cup holders Leeds, see-sawed between the sorry and the spectacular up to Christmas, and ended with the club winning all but three of its 15 final matches. Once again, Roy's side finished in the top four and earned a Championship semi-final match against their previous season's nemesis, Oldham.

It was a match no one expected Hull to win. When the two sides met earlier in April, Hull were crushed 43-9. But Roy had learned some hard lessons quickly. He drew up a plan for his forwards to dominate the game by neutralising Oldham playmakers Frank Pitchford and Derek Turner, and so starve Oldham's backs of the ball. It worked, and by half-time Hull led 18-3. Whiteley comprehensively outplayed Turner, and Pitchford was knocked out in the second half after an altercation with Tommy Harris, who was sent off and banned from playing in the Championship Final. It was the only downside in a performance that saw Hull surge into the final with the wind in their sails.

Their opponents were Workington Town, who finished higher in the league and had been aiming for a league and cup double. The first 25 minutes of the final was ferocious and evenly balanced, but then Workington's key forward, Cec Thompson, awkwardly tackled Hull's Cyril Sykes and severely damaged his knee ligaments.

Without 'their most skilled tactician and ball distributor,' as Thompson was described by *Yorkshire Sports*, Workington had lost the one man who could disrupt Hull's increasingly dominant forward pack.

It was not only the decisive turning point in the match, it was also a pivotal moment in Cec Thompson's rugby league career. Born in Leeds in 1926 to a Trinidadian father and a local white woman, he was fostered out as a baby and then sent to orphanages after his father died and his mother was made homeless. Illiterate when he left school, he found a labouring job in an engineering factory and in 1948 was asked to play for its rugby league team. He never looked back. Less than four years later, he followed Roy and became the second black player to play for Great Britain. He was publicly supported by Eddie Waring, who wrote in his *Sunday Pictorial* column, 'if Cec Thompson is not chosen, the selectors must be racists.' Fast, powerful, and able to dictate the ebb and flow of an attack through his handling skills and leadership abilities, he was never able to throw off the knee injury he picked up in the 1958 Championship final. His playing career ended in 1960, when he became the head coach of Barrow.

Without Thompson, Workington were ripped apart by Hull's faster forwards. Hull scored four tries and it could have been more. 'The open-style classical handling which Roy Francis brought to the Boulevard was too much for a bewildered Workington whose much vaunted defence crumbled gradually and in the end became almost non-existent,' wrote Mike Ackroyd. The celebrations were even sweeter because all of the Hull forwards in the match – for which Welshman Tommy Harris was suspended and the Workington-born Drake brothers were injured – had been born and bred in the city.

Roy was now at the peak of his career. He had proved he was not merely a pioneer or an innovator, but that he was also consistently successful. And in rugby league, as in all professional sport, what mattered more than anything else was winning. His ideas had been vindicated and he had demonstrated that his methods brought results. And somewhere deep down, he no doubt felt that he was repaying all the humiliations, the petty insults, and the racist abuse he and his family had endured. Success was the best revenge.

When the team arrived back at Hull's Guildhall in the city centre after the match, thousands of people were waiting to welcome them home and celebrate their historic triumph. As the players appeared on the balcony overlooking the city's biggest crowd since VE Day, it was Roy everyone wanted to hear. 'The cheering did not die away until coach Roy Francis, beaming with pleasure, went to the microphone to say "thank you very much for such a wonderful reception",' reported the *Hull Daily Mail*.

The crowd would not let him go. He came back to the microphone to thank all the supporters and the back-room staff. And he came back again to announce that an open-top bus parade would travel through the whole city on Monday. He was a victorious returning general, commanding the balcony, and the crowd hung on his every word. Perhaps he was now experiencing the same emotions his father Lionel felt when he had addressed thousands of people at rallies across America in the 1920s and 1930s.

Yet there was one major difference. The crowds whom Lionel had thrilled and excited during his barnstorming days in America were entirely black. But the crowd which clamoured to hear his son was almost entirely white. Roy Francis had become a black leader in a white world.

WEMBLEY: THE OBSESSION

There was one remaining pinnacle for Roy to conquer: Wembley.

It was indisputable that the winner of the Championship final was the best rugby league team of the season. Consisting of 38 matches, a semi-final and the final itself, it was a gruelling, exhausting route march which began in the autumn sunshine, ploughed on through the mud, rain and snow of winter, and ended just as spring was turning into summer. Front-runners faded and dark horses emerged as the sheer length of the season bent, twisted and tested clubs beyond endurance. Like working in a coal mine or on a deep-sea trawler, winning the Championship was about guts, determination, and using your head wisely.

But the Challenge Cup was different. It was about glamour and prestige, knock-out matches and the luck of the draw, where a run of good fortune could bring glory to a town whose team maybe didn't have the resources to compete for the Championship. And the final at Wembley was rugby league's annual day in the sun, the one time of the year that the game was not ignored by the national media. Viewed by the London-based media as a northern game, and sometimes looked down upon by the same people as a working-class sport, league constantly struggled for column inches and airtime. But ever since the cup final was moved to Wembley in 1929, it had been more than just a match. It was a festival of the sport, a celebration of northern England, and an opportunity to demonstrate where the best type of rugby was played. For many thousands of northerners, the pilgrimage to Wembley was the first time they had visited London. The Championship final was anchored in the north, but the winners at Wembley would bask in national glory.

Roy had never played at Wembley. Nor had Hull; their last Challenge Cup final was in 1923, six years before the match was moved to London. During Roy's time as Hull coach, the club had never been within touching distance of the Challenge Cup final. But now, as the champions of rugby league, there could be no doubt that Wembley was Hull's next goal.

That season's league campaign proved to be something of a disappointment. A fixture backlog meant Hull had to play five games in the last 11 days of the regular season, and two losses meant that they narrowly missed out on a place in the top four. But the frenetic last days of the season also saw them defeat Featherstone Rovers in a Challenge Cup semi-final and claim a place at Wembley. What better way to make up for disappointment in the league than a win at Wembley?

The initial preparation for the cup final could not have gone better. Roy planned out a training schedule to allow the team to peak at the right time. On the Sunday before the final, the first team played a practice match against reserve team players, dubbed by the press as 'Hull versus the Rest'. Training sessions were held on the next three days and the team travelled down to Wembley by coach on the Thursday before the match. On the Friday morning, the players went for the traditional pre-match walk around the Wembley pitch before being taken on a coach tour of London's most famous sight-seeing spots.

'Hull will win the Rugby League Challenge Cup at Wembley on Saturday,' the *Hull Daily Mail* confidently predicted on the day the team travelled down to London. The newspaper's front-page headline 'Cup Final Crisis on the Docks' explained that over 2000 dockers wanted to go to Wembley but had been refused permission by the dock employers. 'It is a special and unique occasion,' a union official told the newspaper. 'Men worked overtime and bank holidays voluntarily and a reciprocal gesture would do much to better relations on the docks.' But on the day of the match there were no problems on the riverfront and the dockers took their place at Wembley alongside an estimated 30,000 other fans from the city. Such was the magic of the Challenge Cup final that even supporters of Hull KR made the trip south to watch their local rivals, although their allegiances were ambiguous: 'We think that Wigan will just win,' teenage KR fan Dave Gotts predicted to a reporter.

On the morning of the match Roy took the team for a training session attended by the media at the ground of Hendon soccer club in North London. It was here that a sense of unease emerged. Johnny Whiteley remembered it as a very hot morning – '60- or 70-degree heat' – but Roy insisted on a full workout for the players. 'We didn't go for a loosener, he had us running up and down the field,' Whiteley recalled. 'I had to tell him, "I think we've done enough."' But Roy insisted on completing the training session and 'So by the time we got back to the hotel for lunch, we were late, so we had to rush everything, jump on the bus and get a police escort to Wembley.'

It was to get worse. The kick-off saw things go very badly, very suddenly. Hull conceded the first try to Wigan after just eight minutes, then allowed three more before half-time. All they could manage in response were two penalty goals. When referee Charlie Appleton ended the first-half, Wigan led 20-4 and the match was effectively over. They scored two more tries before Tommy Finn finally crossed the line for Hull with eight minutes to go. No team had ever before scored 30 points in a Challenge Cup final at Wembley. Beaten 30-13, Hull had been humiliated.

'We were pretty tired up to half-time and in the second half we just ran out of steam,' Whiteley lamented. 'We were cocky to an extent where we lost an edge and Wigan on the day were a far superior side.' They had certainly underestimated their opponents' big-match expertise. Wigan were the current cup-holders and were making their sixth appearance at Wembley. But as Whiteley admitted privately, Roy had also miscalculated badly. Maintaining a rigorous training regime up to and including the day of the final simply added to the stress felt by the players as the big match approached. In contrast to Hull's intense build-up, Wigan players went to Blackpool during the week of the final and were then driven down to London the day before the match.

Playing a final at Wembley was an experience like no other in rugby league, something which Whiteley thought Roy did not fully appreciate: 'Roy had never been in a Wembley cup final, so it just shows you that even with all the intelligence and knowledge, you still need a different approach or insight as to how to go about the couple of days before the final.' Whiteley blamed the rigorous pre-match training session at Hendon on Roy's vanity: 'All the press were there because we were there for training. Roy showed off with us. He liked the limelight.'

The team's preparations were also not helped by rumours that Roy would be leaving Hull to coach Halifax. In April, the *Daily Mirror* reported that Roy was in talks with Halifax about joining them for the next season. At the same time, it was revealed that he and Rene were also moving out of their Cross Keys pub in Beverley, suggesting that the speculation might have some substance. The Hull directors scotched the rumour, but on the morning of the cup final they felt obliged to issue another denial. In fact, on the Thursday after the cup final Roy met with Halifax officials, who offered him a 'four-figure' salary. The following week, Halifax coach Gareth Price was sacked. Faced with the imminent loss of the architect of their success, the Hull directors offered Roy what the press termed 'certain supplementary improvements' to his contract, and he finally turned down the Halifax offer.

Recommitted to Hull, Roy seemed to overcome the Wembley embarrassment and the club started the 1959–60 season on fire. They reached the final of the Yorkshire Cup in October but lost by a solitary point to Featherstone Rovers. As usual, Roy's carefully-prepared training regime meant the club began to peak in the second half of the season. They lost just three of their final 23 matches, and the usual manic last weeks of the season saw them play nine matches in April. They finished third in the league to qualify for the Championship semi-finals again and also reached the Challenge Cup final at Wembley for the second successive season. Statistically, it was the most successful season in Hull's history.

And then came April, the cruellest month, when the grinding effects of playing two games a week shattered the Hull team. By coincidence, their third-place finish in the league meant they had to travel to Wakefield Trinity for the Championship semi-final, just a week before they would play each other at Wembley. Wakefield were an increasingly dominant team, thanks to their brutally unforgiving forward pack, led by Derek Turner, and a mesmerising back line starring the sublimely skilled Neil Fox. In the semi-final they took Hull by the throat and squeezed until they emerged as 24-4 victors.

Local rugby league lore had it that Wakefield had deliberately tried to injure Hull players before the Wembley showdown. Full-back Peter Bateson was badly concussed due to a late tackle by Turner, and further collateral damage meant that three of Hull's three-quarter line were also rendered incapable of playing in the cup final. Whatever had happened in that match, the accumulated injury toll from April meant that half of the club's powerhouse forward pack – Cyril Sykes and Jim and Bill Drake – were also unlikely to play again that season. Wembley was just seven days away, and Roy knew that injuries meant it was unlikely that he could select a strong team.

Two days before the cup final, the *Hull Daily Mail* published pen portraits of the 17 players in Hull's cup final squad. Only nine of the profiled players would actually walk out at Wembley. Five automatic first-teamers could not play due to injury and key squad members such as Peter Whiteley, Johnny's brother, and backs Arthur Keegan and Brian Saville were also out. Roy had so few fit players that he was forced to pick second-row forward Mike Smith, who never even played for the first team after only just signing for Hull. Smith became the first professional player in either rugby or soccer to make his first-team debut in a Wembley cup final.

'We still have a few aces up our sleeves,' Johnny Whiteley optimistically told the press as the team left for Wembley, but a sense of foreboding accompanied the thousands of Hull supporters travelling south to watch their team. The memory of last year's collapse against Wigan was still raw. Yet at half-time, Wakefield led by a mere seven points to five. Perhaps a miracle could happen?

It didn't. In fact, Hull endured one of the worst halves of rugby the club had ever experienced, conceding five tries as Wakefield piled up 31 unanswered points. Ron Cowan broke a rib scoring Hull's only try, Whiteley was temporarily knocked out by a punch, and Tommy Harris was so badly concussed after a tackle he was hospitalised. The only consolation was that Harris's performance was so heroic that he won the Lance Todd Trophy for the player of the match. He spoke for the team when he later told the press, 'I feel sorry for coach Roy Francis. ... [winning at Wembley] has been an obsession for him for a year.'

TORMENT

In sport, as in life, it is always difficult to pinpoint the precise moment that a relationship begins to break down. A second successive humiliation at Wembley weighed heavily on an intensely ambitious and hugely proud man like Roy. On the surface, the defeat did not change his relationship with the club, but he realised it would take a tremendous effort to restore pride and self-belief in a now-ageing team. Nevertheless, for most of the following season they remained in contention for a top-four spot in the league and reached the Challenge Cup semi-final.

But something had changed. The buoyant confidence of the team and its supporters was ebbing away. Few expected them to overcome St Helens in the Cup semi-final and no one was surprised when they were beaten 20-9. And whereas Roy always prided himself on being able to get Hull to peak at the business end of the season, this one spluttered out with a string of defeats. They even lost the Easter Monday derby match against a newly resurgent Hull KR, coached by Roy's protégé Colin Hutton, the first time they had lost to their cross-town rivals since 1955.

There was no decisive breaking point in Roy's relationship with the club. It just slowly unravelled over time. As his team grew older, Roy and the club's supporters grew frustrated with the directors' refusal to buy quality players to renew the side. By 1961 the consensus was the forwards were too old and the backs were too slow, yet the club continued to rely on its 'golden generation' of forwards and the directors insisted that the policy of recruiting local players would eventually unearth match-winners. The club's only significant signings were future Great Britain captain Clive Sullivan, although his talent would only truly flower later in the mid-1960s, and the former Springbok rugby union winger Wilf Rosenberg. Both made their debuts in the same match, with Sullivan picking up a hat-trick and Rosenberg touching down twice.

Although Rosenberg was a white South African, Roy did not experience the problems he had with Pin McMillan. Having played two seasons with Leeds, Rosenberg would have been well aware of Roy Francis. It may have also made a difference that Rosenberg was Jewish. In Hull, the game was the sport of choice of the local Jewish community, most of whom traced their roots to families who fled Tsarist persecution in Russia in the 1890s and 1900s. Tens of thousands had passed through the port of Hull en route to America, but some had stayed in the city. In the 1920s Hull KR had a Jewish captain, Louis Harris, who later became a director of the club. He was followed on to the board by his nephew Max Gold, who went on to become the club chairman. In the 1950s the Hull Schools' rugby league trophy was named the Coupland Cup in honour of Maurice Coupland, a local businessman well-known for his love of the game. One synagogue in the city even had an informal rule that Hull and Hull KR fans had to sit on opposite sides of the congregation.

When talk in the synagogue turned to rugby, just as in the pubs and clubs, Hull supporters were agreed that having Rosenberg and Sullivan served little purpose if the ball was not passed to them often enough, Moreover, the directors made little attempt to rebuild what was now an ageing pack of forwards. Results declined so badly that when the Rugby Football League split the league into two divisions in 1962, Hull finished one place above the relegation zone.

Although Roy signed a new four-year contract in May 1961, there were hints that he was perhaps losing interest after more than 12 years at the club. Six months earlier he obtained a British Boxing Board of Control licence to train boxers, and he briefly became a trainer to Johnny Halafihi. A few days after signing the new Hull contract he unexpectedly flew to Berlin as part of Halafihi's training team for a bout against the German boxer Helmut Ballr. Questions were asked if Roy was getting bored with rugby, but in fact there was something more fundamental going on. A few days after getting back from Germany, Rene took Roy to University College Hospital in London to undergo psychiatric treatment.

Ian Francis first noticed his father's problem a few weeks earlier. 'He was walking down the street towards me, and I said, "Hello, Dad," but he just walked past me, Ian said. 'He looked at me but just shot daggers at me. He was having a nervous breakdown.'

Roy was taken into the care of Dr Desmond Pond, one of the founders of modern psychiatry in Britain who would shortly become the first professor of psychiatry in London. Dr Pond admitted Roy as an in-patient at the hospital and he spent around three weeks being treated. Rene later said that Pond told her that he'd never met such a complicated man as Roy. 'He's just like an onion. You peel away one layer and then you've got to get through another one,' he explained to her. When Roy was discharged, the couple went on holiday to Mallorca but on their first day there Roy was thrown from a scooter he was driving and spent eight days in a Palma hospital recovering from severe bruising and abrasions. It was not the best of summers.

At such a distance from today, it is impossible to know what triggered Roy's nervous collapse. Mental health issues are invariably complex and multi-faceted, and we can never fully understand the lived experiences of another person. He was approaching middle age and his two sons were now adults, a major transitional point in anyone's life. The change in family life which he valued so much took its toll, and at one point Roy and Rene had made plans, ultimately unsuccessful, to adopt two young black children. Moreover, the failure in two Wembley cup finals must have shaken his self-confidence, and the Hull directors' refusal to enter the transfer market and rebuild their ageing team chafed against his unquenched ambition. His attempt to become a boxing trainer may have been a signal that he was searching for another outlet for his talent. The upwards arc of the rugby career he had pursued since he was 17 seemed to have reached a plateau.

However, countless other people have experienced similar and worse events as middle age crept up on them but not experienced such a profound mental crisis. But Roy was unlike other people in Britain at that time: he was a black leader in an overwhelmingly white world. Peter Roe, the Bradford Northern player and himself a future coach, became close to Roy in the 1970s and came to understand the struggles he had faced in his life. 'He had his demons,' explained Peter, 'he suffered terribly from racism.' Roy's creation of a team with a family spirit, where respect was due and given to all, was not simply a way to win rugby matches. It was also a way to create an environment that protected him from racism. Inside that team which he controlled and shaped, he could be certain there would be no racial insults, no 'casual racism' and no disrespect.

But outside of this world, he could be certain of nothing. He couldn't enter a hotel without worrying he might be turned away. He couldn't run a business without fear of being discriminated against. He couldn't even have a carefree walk with his wife during the evening without the knowledge that they could be insulted in the street. In rugby league he was an undisputed and deeply respected leader of men; outside of it, he was just another black man.

In this, Roy's life was not dissimilar to those of black American jazz musicians whose artistry and expertise made them some of the greatest musical artists of the 20th century. But when they stepped off the stage or out of the concert, they were deprived of the respect and authority they had acquired. Perhaps the most notorious example of this took place in August 1959 when Miles Davis was headlining at the famous Birdland jazz club in New York. Between sets he stepped outside for a cigarette and a policeman told him to move on. When Miles pointed to his name on the billboards, he was arrested and beaten up. No matter how successful they were, a black person was never far from humiliation.

Like Miles, many musicians tried to escape the dehumanising effects of this world through drugs. Roy drank, but not enough to immunise him from the effects of racism. The contradiction between his high status in rugby league and the lack of status in the outside world eventually took its toll on his mental health. 'No black man can hope ever to be entirely liberated from this internal warfare,' commented black American writer James Baldwin in 1953. Medical research in London as early as 1965 found that people from a Caribbean background were almost 40 per cent more likely to experience 'conspicuous psychiatric morbidity' than white Britons. Even today, black people are nine times more likely to be living with schizophrenia. Even a man of Roy's extraordinary presence of mind and self-confidence could not free himself of the everyday fear of humiliation and the need to be steeled against it every single day of his life.

Although Roy seems to have made a full recovery, it did little to reconcile him to Hull. Soon after the new season kicked off, he

missed a Hull reserve team match and was spotted sitting alongside
Barrow coach Cec Thompson during his club's match at Hull KR.
Although Roy defended himself by saying that Thompson had
invited him, the fact that he was watching Hull KR instead of his
own club infuriated many Hull fans. Then, in December 1962,
Hull supporters who travelled to their game at Warrington were
startled to read in the match-day programme that 'Roy Francis will
be leaving at the end of the season ... and we understand that he
may be returning to Lancashire'. Although Hull chairman Ernie
Hardaker denied any such thing, it seemed to be one more step
towards the inevitable.

In May 1963 it became clear that the writing was truly on the
wall when Roy announced he was moving to Dewsbury to take over
a pub, The Whistler. Running a pub almost 60 miles away while
still coaching in Hull would be almost impossible. Roy told the
club he would be in the city only on match days and Tuesday and
Thursday training sessions. He also announced he was abandoning
his famed summer training sessions, which he had always claimed
were the secret to his players' superior fitness during the season.
Although the players wanted to continue, he told the press he
had decided on a complete shutdown, which meant 'we will all
come back fresh to the game, a good deal heavier of course, but
with all deep-seated bruises completely cleared up'. This sounded
somewhat self-serving and contributed to the fans' frustration at
the club's annual general meeting in July. When Ernie Hardaker
told critics of the team's tactics that the players were 'playing to the
coach's instructions' a ripple of applause broke out when someone
heckled, 'Let's get another coach then.' To criticise Roy like that
was once unthinkable, but by now the emotional bond which held
the coach, the club and the supporters together had worn thin by
a lack of success.

Although we have no way of knowing for certain, the evidence
suggests Roy had wanted to leave Hull for some time. By moving to
Dewsbury, in the heart of West Yorkshire's rugby league stronghold,
Roy was putting himself on the market. The move away from Hull
and the scaling down of day-to-day coaching duties seem to have

been a passive-aggressive stance which he hoped would force Hull to release him from his contract.

The decisive moment came on the last Wednesday of October 1963. Early that morning Johnny Whiteley took a telephone call from Roy, asking him to come to the ground urgently. 'I went down there on my bike,' Johnny remembered. 'I went into his office and he said, "I'm leaving you, I'm going to Leeds. You're the new coach." And he gave me his whistle. I walked out of there as Hull's new coach.'

A few hours later, people going home from work on a damp autumn evening found themselves confronted with the *Hull Daily Mail*'s front-page headline 'Quick Move After Francis Bombshell: Johnny Whiteley Hull's New Coach'. And when they turned to the back page, its headline confirmed this was the end of an era: 'Link with Hull's Glorious Years Severed'.

After 14 years as the King of West Hull, Roy Francis was leaving to become coach of Leeds.

7

Glory and its Complications:
1963–1968

'The final act is down to you. You are all prepared,
you are all good enough.'

When Roy arrived in Leeds in November 1963 he stepped onto the biggest stage of his career. Leeds was a big city, more than twice the size of Hull and significantly larger than anywhere else in rugby league. It was the financial and cultural capital of Yorkshire which, as its citizens proudly knew, was the biggest county in Britain. Although the city had historically been portrayed as one of the grimiest, dirtiest examples of the industrial revolution – Charles Dickens described it as 'odious and beastly' – Roy's arrival coincided with its emergence as one of the centres of the northern artistic renaissance of the 1960s.

Local boy and childhood rugby league player Peter O'Toole had just been nominated for an Oscar for his performance in *Lawrence of Arabia*. Former Leeds rugby league 'A' team player David Storey was the toast of the literary world for his novel, and screenplay of, *This Sporting Life*. The film of Hunslet-born Keith Waterhouse's best-selling *Billy Liar* had been released a few weeks before Roy's arrival, and Richard Hoggart's book *The Uses of Literacy* had almost single-handedly begun the study of working-class life. In cricket, Headingley-based Yorkshire had begun a domination of the county championship that lasted throughout the 1960s, while the appointment of the innovative Don Revie as manager of the traditionally underperforming Leeds United in 1961 signalled the start of a new era for soccer in the city. In 1963 Leeds was a city with a spring in its step.

It was also a city of immigrants. It provided refuge to tens of thousands of Irish people fleeing the famine in Ireland in the 1840s and 1850s, and 50 years later became home to thousands of Jews escaping anti-semitic pogroms in the Tsar's Russia. Michael Marks, the founder of Marks & Spencer, and Montague Burton, who brought smart tailoring to the masses, were both immigrants who started their business empires in the city. By the early 1960s a new wave of arrivals from the Caribbean and the Indian sub-continent were also making new lives in Leeds. Symbolising the changing times, in 1961 the rugby league side signed the forward Louie Neumann from a South African 'Coloured' rugby union club in Western Province, and Leeds United recruited winger Albert Johanneson from South African soccer that same year.

This new wave of immigration contributed to a sense that Leeds was changing rapidly. Slum clearances over the previous decade and heavy investment in new roads to accommodate the revolution in car ownership of the late 1950s and 1960s had transformed the face of the city. Built on a tricornered foundation of mining, engineering, and woollen-cloth manufacture, the decline of the coal and textile industry left many of Leeds' traditional working-class areas struggling to survive. To the south of the city, Hunslet saw its population almost halved between 1951 and 1981, and from being a rugby league powerhouse, its local club faced the 1970s bankrupt and homeless.

Hunslet's fall from grace contrasted sharply with the rise of its rugby rivals in North Leeds. Based in the comfortable suburb of Headingley, Leeds rugby league club was historically the richest club in rugby league. This was partly due to its ownership of the Headingley cricket and rugby ground, which meant that income from Test match cricket provided a handsome subsidy for the club, but also because it still retained support from some of the local business and professional classes who elsewhere had largely abandoned the sport after the 1895 rugby split. This also meant the club felt it had a certain status to maintain and so expected to be regularly competing for the top honours in the game.

This level of ambition – or hubris, as its rivals believed – matched Roy's. At Leeds, he would not be frustrated by the directors' unwillingness to recruit top players, as he had been at Hull. Leeds felt no restraints about using its money to bring the best talent to Headingley, whether from rival clubs, overseas rugby league, or rugby union. In 1952 it had paid a massive £6,000 to Lewis Jones, the golden boy of Welsh rugby union, for him to switch to league. They were so enthusiastic to bring his prodigious talent to Leeds that they failed to check the club's bank balance before recruiting him, and the signing-on cheque bounced.

The signing of Lewis Jones was perhaps the best example of Leeds' commitment to playing rugby with style. Its supporters and officials believed rugby should be played in an open and flowing fashion, with backs who were fleet of foot, sure of hand, and capable of scoring tries from anywhere on the pitch. God forbid their team would ever be tempted to engage in dour forward battles or that the ball spent more time being kicked instead of being passed. Leeds' belief that the manner of victory was as important as the victory itself was spelt out by the Leeds directors to a bemused Willie Davies, two days after he had captained the club to its first-ever Yorkshire Cup final win in 1921. The club minutes record how Davies was called before the directors to defend himself from their accusations that the team had engaged in 'an excess of kicking' in the final, contrary to the club's playing philosophy. Although he would have rankled at such blatant interference by directors, Roy fully shared their commitment to open rugby.

THE REBUILDING STRATEGY

Roy arrived at Leeds during a period of transition for the team. The players who won the Challenge Cup at Wembley in 1957 and the club's first-ever Championship trophy in 1961 were slowly fading from the scene. Leeds needed a coach to rebuild the team on the right basis. Roy's old friend Trevor Foster, the former Bradford, Wales and Great Britain international, had been the coach since 1962 but had never been seen as more than a stop-gap, and there was no ill-feeling between the two men when Roy came in.

He began by focusing on the fitness of players. Just as at Hull, each player was given a pair of running spikes. 'Everything has to be done at pace, I want fast rugby,' teenage scrum-half Barry Seabourne remembered Roy telling the squad just after he arrived. Winger Alan Smith, another recent teenage recruit, was shocked at the intensity of the training: 'We lapped the outer perimeter of the cricket field so many times, then Roy mapped out 400 yards on the pitch and divided the squad into smaller teams, each with an equal number of backs and forwards,' he said. 'It was so hard it made us physically sick.' There were various types of shuttle-training where players would run in teams to complete 16 sprints over 150 yards. Roy also devised a stamina programme in which the players would continuously run around a circuit of Headingley's cricket and rugby pitches and up and down the steps of the stands. 'Roy trained us like athletes rather than rugby players,' recalled Scottish centre-three quarter Drew Broatch. 'We were superbly fit.'

There were no shortcuts to the excellence he demanded. Players who tried to cut corners or cheated on the long, energy-sapping runs around the stadium complex were soon spotted by Ernie Seabourne, one of Roy's assistants and Barry's father. 'At the end of the day, lads, you're going to hate my guts; and that's the way I want it,' Roy told his players before one early training session. But they didn't hate him. The new regime did shake out some of the older players who couldn't or wouldn't reach the fitness levels he demanded, but the sheer professionalism of his approach endeared him to the new generation. At one point Roy gathered together all of the club's young players, most of whom were still in their teens, and told them: 'I'm going to get you fit and show you how to play the game because you're going to be the future of this club, but you have to work hard to achieve that.' And they all did.

But they were still no match yet for tough, mature teams like Wigan or Wakefield Trinity. Rebuilding had to be done in stages, with temporary supports being brought in to strengthen the structures inside which tomorrow's players could be nurtured. Unlike at Hull, Leeds gave Roy responsibility for signing players and this enabled him to bring in experienced men who could provide some of the backbone around which he could build. To strengthen the forwards, he brought in tried and tested players like Bill Drake, one of the rocks of his great Hull pack, along with hooker Alan Lockwood from Dewsbury. The backs were given extra style and steel with the acquisition of the Hull centre Dick Gemmell. The combination of players at the end of their careers and others just starting out, with little in between, was not immediately successful and Leeds finished 13th in the league.

It was only in the summer of 1964 that Roy could really start his rebuilding project. He began pre-season training in July, well before the season kicked off. Dick Gemmell, who had experienced Roy's pre-season training sessions at Hull, warned his new teammates that 'you're all in for a big surprise'. He was right; it was unlike anything the Leeds players had ever experienced. 'Wow! It was like this is a different world,' remembered Phil Holmes, another of Leeds' prodigiously talented teenagers. 'The first day of training we got a new pair of boots. But with Roy, there were two boxes of boots – one of them was a pair of spikes. He had everything to the nth degree, always. As soon as you'd start training, he'd say, "Right, you're not going to see a ball for a couple of weeks. We're going to get to a level, as they do in athletics, where you reach a peak and then every week we'll keep that peak level of fitness topped up."'

It started to pay dividends. Leeds began to climb the league ladder and at the end of October 1964 they reached the Yorkshire Cup final, where they met Wakefield Trinity, the side which had become Roy's nemesis. Getting to the final showed how far Leeds had progressed in Roy's first year, but playing in the final highlighted how much further they had to go. They were outclassed by the customary brilliance of Wakefield's backs and the impermeable toughness of its forwards. Leeds ended the season tenth in the league, higher than the previous season but not good enough for the club, its fans or Roy. Rebuilding still had a long way to go.

Despite their instinctive skills, youthful fitness and tireless appetite for the game, Leeds' young players still lacked the maturity and 'nous' – the experience that provides the ability to make the right decision at the right time – that the very best teams had. Ken Eyre, a vastly experienced forward signed from Hunslet, recounted that Roy told him 'he had to buy some time. He was more excited about the potential he could see in the second team but he couldn't bring it through all at once'. So he strengthened the leadership of the team with experienced players like Eyre, Great Britain loose-forward Harry Poole from Hull KR, and scrum-half Ken Rollin, one of the architects of Wakefield's demolition of Hull in the 1960 Challenge Cup final.

The signing of Rollin was controversial. He had actually retired from playing and would temporarily replace the up-and-coming Barry Seabourne in the scrum-half position. In many teams Seabourne would have taken offence and demanded a transfer, but Roy took the 18-year-old to one side and explained his reasons. 'I'm buying Rollin just for this season to give you time to learn the game and improve in the "A" team,' Barry remembered Roy telling him. 'I want you to learn every time you play, to look and think, and see what's happening.' Reassured, Seabourne accepted the coach's decision and his advice. Although he didn't know it at the time, he was being groomed by Roy to be the future playmaker and captain of the club.

As at Hull, Roy and Rene also worked hard at creating a warm and supportive atmosphere for the Leeds players and their families. 'Roy was good with all the wives, he was always conscious of keeping people together,' explained Margaret Dewhurst, wife of full-back Robin Dewhurst. 'Roy once said to me,' recalled Val Broatch, 'if you keep the players' wives happy, you keep the players happy. And he did a lot for the wives, he encouraged them to feel part of the team. He organised a players' bar, for the wives basically. He wanted everyone to feel part of a family.' Her husband Drew also pointed out that, 'That was a big thing for Roy. He really concentrated on the family side of it. He made sure that everyone was happy and enjoying it, and that you didn't feel under pressure.'

After matches, players and their wives would be invited to Roy's pub, The Whistler, where he hosted a lock-in session – where drinks were served after the legal closing time – for them all. These were not hard-drinking sessions but fun evenings where Roy would lead the singing – 'I Am The Music Man' and 'Keep Right On To The End Of The Road' were two of his favourites – and the proceedings would end about 1.30 in the morning after Rene had made bacon and egg sandwiches for everyone. Alternatively, after home matches, there would be a players' and wives' lock-in at the bar at Headingley stadium, which would culminate in 30-odd fish and chip suppers being ordered by Roy.

Rene never missed a Leeds match and would encourage all the players' wives and girlfriends to go. She was the unofficial organiser of the female half of the team. If a young woman didn't know anything about rugby, Rene sat next to her and explained what was going on. If a player and his wife were facing difficult times personally, Roy and Rene would take time to visit them and offer support. Although Roy's 'happy wife, happy life' policy was ultimately about creating a successful rugby team, Rene also encouraged women to play an active role in the team culture.

When Roy made Barry Seabourne the team captain, Rene encouraged his wife Janice to think of herself as 'the captain's wife' and pushed her to speak in public and see herself as the leader of the wives and girlfriends. Rene would also arrange nights out for them at pubs and restaurants, so they could socialise outside of the rugby environment. Their joint role in building a team culture was almost unique. 'I don't think I ever spoke to any other coaches when Barry was playing,' recalled Janice. 'No one else involved you. Whatever things went on, wives weren't involved, it was a male-only thing. I can't remember speaking to any other coach apart from Roy.'

This nurturing culture was a precious commodity for Roy and Rene, and Roy strongly resisted outside disruptions to his team. This became apparent in October 1965 when Robin Dewhurst fell victim to his recurring knee problem, and the Leeds directors invited the Australian Ken Thornett to come to play for the club during the Australian off-season. Thornett was the full-back in Leeds' championship-winning team of 1961 and was very popular among Leeds fans. However, the directors' decision did not go down well with Roy. Signing players on short-term contracts did not fit his long-term perspective of team rebuilding, which was based on settled players with shared goals and culture. Parachuting-in a player for part of the season disrupted that process. Moreover, the gifted Thornett was a happy-go-lucky character who was probably closer in temperament to the carefree amateur ethos of rugby union at the time – his brother John captained Australia's rugby union side – than to the professionalism demanded by Roy. When Thornett and Roy met for the first time in a local pub, the Australian later described it as a three-hour interview. 'I found it a little bit hard with Roy,' he explained. 'I suppose it was a bit awkward coming in but I don't think he was that keen on me coming back ... I wasn't there for the full period and so he felt that that'd be an unnerving effect on the players who were just coming in.'

Roy's frustration at the Thornett signing was made worse because he had wanted to sign the Leigh full-back Bev Risman, the son of Roy's former Dewsbury teammate Gus Risman and a former England and British Lions rugby union player. As Thornett's English sojourn came to an end and there was no sign of Dewhurst's injuries abating, the Leeds directors finally acceded to Roy and signed Risman at the start of 1966. This solved the full-back problem, gave Leeds a highly reliable goal-kicker, and added considerable experience to the team. The move was not unproblematic for Risman, however. He was taken aback at his first training session under Roy: 'I had always been an enthusiastic and dedicated trainer, and with my PE teaching background I thought I knew what it was all about, but was not prepared for what was to come,' he remembered. 'I was nowhere near his required fitness levels and my first few weeks were spent trying to improve my speed and stamina to cope with [Roy's] demands.'

Thornett was noteworthy for being one of the few players who didn't get on with Roy. Even Dewhurst, whose brilliance was frustrated by injuries which cut short his Leeds' career, never changed his positive opinion: 'I thought he was a fabulous coach. Way beyond his time.' Although much of Roy's success as a coach was due to what he had learned in the Army Physical Training Corps, he also had the psychological skills to instil self-confidence in his players. 'He had a way of getting the best out of young players by kidding us along,' said the future Leeds captain and coach Syd Hynes. Dewhurst recalled how 'when he'd finish talking to you, you'd think bloody hell, what a good player I am'. His ability to instil self-confidence in players, to respect themselves and those around them, was noted by almost all of those who played for him: 'He gave you the confidence to do things. As a player, if someone gives you that confidence you're going to do a little bit better, and you're going to try a little bit harder.'

Empowering his players was at the heart of the way he wanted Leeds to play. He did not prepare a game plan or detail specific tactics for matches. Playmakers like Seabourne would be encouraged to make their own tactical decisions as the match developed. In some ways his sides appeared to play a very simple type of rugby, which was summed up by Robin Dewhurst as 'when you get the ball, move it from one side to the other, and the gaps will appear'. His training regime meant that Leeds were so fit that they would invariably pull away from tiring opponents in the last 10 minutes of matches.

But there was more to how Leeds played rugby than ball movement and sheer speed. After each tackle, the team would set up in an arrow formation, with ball distributors on both sides of the play-the-ball. Tackled players had to spring up quickly from a tackle so the hooker could get the ball smoothly to the players standing 20 yards outside of him, who then moved the ball further out wide. At the next tackle the ball would be swung the opposite way. If a gap didn't always appear in the opponents' defensive line, such rapid movement would usually fatigue defenders, causing them to miss tackles on Leeds ball-carriers.

'Our only instructions were to play when the opportunity arose and react to situations as they came up,' winger John Atkinson later told rugby league writer Phil Caplan. 'If an opponent was running through a particular hole, then we knew we had to adjust to close it.' In defence, players were encouraged to talk to each other and respond to where the attackers were standing. The side would use what would later become known as an 'umbrella defence' in which the defenders would rush up in the shape of an open umbrella, cutting off access to the outside attackers and forcing their opponents to move the ball back into the middle of the pitch, where the Leeds forwards would cut them down. Roy's defensive watchwords were fitness, intensity and self-confidence, just as in attack.

By the spring of 1966 his rebuilding plan was beginning to show results. Leeds finished sixth in the league, their highest position since being champions in 1961, and came within a converted try of realising the Wembley dream. After winning a replayed quarter-final with Warrington, they came face-to-face with Roy's other bogey team, Wigan, in the semi-final. In a hard attritional game, Wigan's greater experience and defensive steel eventually won out 7-2, thanks to a solitary Billy Boston try. Despite the disappointment, Roy was satisfied and consoled the team with the thought that they weren't ready for the final because they were not yet strong enough. The memory of Hull's awful defeat at Wembley in 1960 still loomed large in his mind. If Leeds were to get to Wembley, Roy wanted them to do so from a position of strength.

RACE AND RESPECT

Roy's ability to get the best out of his players and weld them into an effective team was ultimately down to the force of his personality. Janice Seabourne, who knew him from 1968 when she first met her future husband Barry, described his personal charisma: 'Roy was someone you should listen to. He was quite wise. He had authority without you really knowing why. He could hold a room. It's something you can't put a finger on but you know when someone has got it.'

The key to his authority was mutual respect. 'The biggest thing about Roy was that he had great respect from his players,' remembered Drew Broatch, 'and not many coaches get that.' Some of that respect came from the fact he never expected players to do anything he was not prepared to do himself. Robin Dewhurst remembered a particularly tough Leeds training session when one player complained that Roy couldn't do what he was telling the players to do. 'He said to Roy, "I'll race you." So Roy said, "All right, go on then," and Roy left him for dead. And he was 48 years old by then, so that quietened down a lot of the lads, who thought "this bloke knows what he's doing."' Roy also made a point of never humiliating or belittling a player, and always avoided, in the vernacular of the dressing room, 'bollocking' players when they made mistakes or played below their abilities.

Roy's emphasis on mutual respect was unusual in an era where coaches in rugby league and soccer would still regularly bawl out players or try to intimidate them into playing better. His understanding of human psychology partly came from his training as an Army PT Instructor, but it was also derived from something more fundamental to his character and upbringing. Throughout his life in South Wales, Roy's father, Lionel Francis, sought respect as a black man living in a white world. Sometimes he found it, such as when he worked as a miner or as a preacher, but mostly his life until he left for America was a fight against employers, landlords and racists for a basic level of human dignity and respect. As well as his experiences growing up in Brynmawr, Roy had also faced disrespectful racist behaviour towards him, such as Harry Sunderland forcing him out of Wigan in 1938 or the Leicester rugby union turnstile operators refusing to let him into the stadium for a wartime England services international.

This withholding of dignity and respect is at the dehumanising core of racism. When the modern slave trade began in the 1600s and 1700s, African people were portrayed as non-human to justify them being captured and traded. The idea that black people did not deserve respect and could be humiliated and stripped of their dignity was a consequence of slavery, but it remained commonplace in the British media and education system. Roy's experiences led him to create a world around him which shielded him from threats to his self-respect. And his players and their families were part of that world. In this world – as it should have been in the outside world but wasn't – everyone was entitled to respect. In short, Roy's success as a coach was ultimately based on the principle of respecting human dignity.

This explains why so many of his players and their wives could say that race was never an issue in their relationship with Roy. As Phil Holmes explained, 'Never, ever did I think anybody degraded him or thought anything about his colour. I never heard anyone say anything about his colour or even be critical about him. He was basically a god. You respected him. When you met him it was like, "I've got Roy talking to me."' As in Hull, Roy became completely accepted at Leeds as the black leader of white people, something unprecedented in 1960s Britain.

When they looked back, many of those who knew Roy in the 1950s and 1960s said they didn't think of him as being black. When Johnny Whiteley's wife Joan was in Hull's Cottingham Road maternity hospital just after giving birth to their first baby, the nurse came round to her and said, 'There's someone to see you; they're black!' 'And Joan said, "I don't know any black people." She'd never seen Roy as black,' said Johnny. In one sense, this appears to deny Roy part of his identity, but it was also a rejection of the racial stereotypes of black people which were appearing in the media at that time. The black person Johnny and Joan Whiteley knew had nothing in common with newspaper depictions of black people as being uncivilised and alien. Growing up and being educated in a virtually all-white environment meant many working-class people had no alternative views of non-white people until they met and worked alongside them. The idea that people 'did not see race' – which in the 21st century is a phrase used to deny the existence of racism – could mean the opposite in the 1950s and 1960s, when racist attitudes were overt and expected to be the norm. And, as could be seen in the Army's colour bar and covertly in many other walks of life, racial stereotypes decreed that black people were incapable of being leaders. Those men and women who accepted Roy as an authority figure were at odds with the prevailing racist stereotypes.

This acceptance was helped by rugby league's egalitarian ethos. Although the sport's authorities had subverted this tradition with its treatment of George Bennett in 1936 and Billy Boston in 1957, the idea that the league judged people on merit alone ran deep in the everyday culture of the game. Television presenter Eddie Waring was fond of describing the sport as 'the most democratic in the world' and, if not always honoured, this spirit was felt wherever it was played. These attitudes had their roots in everyday working-class life. In World War Two, black American GIs in Britain often remarked that they felt more accepted by working-class people than by other classes. Paul Robeson, the black American actor and singer, became a folk hero to many miners in South Wales through his concerts and the 1940 film, *The Proud Valley*, in which he starred as a black miner. Looking back on the 1950s when he played professional soccer in the North of England, Australian Aboriginal activist Charles Perkins felt that industrial workers shared similar problems to people of colour. Even at the most informal of levels, small acts of everyday humanity often occurred. Charlie Williams remembered times when, as the only black person at dances in the 1940s, white girls would ignore racist taunts to dance with him, and other occasions when 'two of us asked two girls to dance and [if] I got turned down, my mate would say, "Sorry, love, but if your friend won't dance with Charlie, I'm not dancing with you."'

In the 1960s racism in Britain became sharper and more overt than it had been during Roy's time in Hull in the 1950s. In Leeds, Afro-Caribbean and Asian immigration to the city in the 1960s was seized upon to justify discrimination and stereotyping. Media outcries about 'unlimited immigration' and so-called 'no-go zones' led to new restrictions on people entering Britain from

Commonwealth countries, fascist groups being given a new lease of life, and politicians seeking to capitalise on racism. It would not be surprising if some players were not influenced by this racism, but every member of Roy Francis' teams accepted his authority. Although he took no interest in politics, Roy's career and the acceptance he found were a direct personal challenge to racism.

WEMBLEY AND COMPLICATED GLORY

In the autumn of 1966, two months into a new season, the nature of rugby league changed and turbo-charged the ascension of Leeds to the very highest peaks of the sport.

Throughout its history, the sport had been bedevilled by the fact that possession of the ball could be monopolised by one team. If a side decided not to pass or kick, the ball could simply be picked up after each tackle and the ball-carrier would run until tackled, and so on, *ad infinitum*. Because there was no limit to the number of times a side could be tackled while in possession of the ball, their opponents could be completely deprived of the ball. Called the 'creeping barrage', it was a tactic that could reduce rugby to tedious barging. After years of discussion and experimentation to solve the problem, eventually the game decided to take a leaf from American football. In October 1966, the rules were changed to that teams could only keep the ball for four tackles. If they did not score after those four tackles, a scrum would take place.

The impact was stunning. Now that teams could not endlessly keep the ball, they were forced to use it or lose it. The game instantly became more open, exciting and free-scoring. The new rule was made for teams which played fast, attacking rugby; teams like Roy Francis' Leeds. Not surprisingly, Roy was a huge fan of the change. 'I love it,' he exclaimed, pointing out that it gave opportunities for 'more variation with the accent on mobility in the forwards'.

Leeds had already made an unbeaten start to the 1966–67 season when the new rule was introduced. Roy's prediction that it would 'make players use their brains more' was vindicated as team after team was torn apart by Leeds' electric passing and instinctive combination play. They ended the season at the top of the league, unbeaten at their Headingley home. Less than four years after he had arrived, Roy had made good on his promise to restore Leeds' place in rugby league's elite.

At the same time that Roy's rugby league team was bringing glory to the city of Leeds, so too was Don Revie's Leeds United. The predecessor of United, Leeds City, had begun life as Holbeck rugby league club, but its failure to be promoted to the top division meant they abandoned rugby for soccer in 1904. For most of its history United remained a middling sort of team until Revie became manager in March 1961. In his first full season as manager United avoided relegation from the Football League's Second Division only by winning the last match of the season, but in 1964 they won promotion to the top flight. The next season they finished runners-up in both the First Division and the FA Cup, and in 1969 Revie's crowning glory came when they were crowned champions for the first time in the club's history. Football's global reach also meant that Revie's side became the face of the city around the world, especially after they became the first British side to win the European Fairs Cup competition in 1968.

Like Roy, Don Revie was an innovator and a leader of men, on and off the pitch. He had pioneered the deep-lying centre forward position as a player and he showed a similarly inventive spirit as a manager. He changed United's strip from blue and amber (the same as the rugby club) to all-white, in emulation of the great Real Madrid side which dominated the European Cup in its early years, and compiled detailed dossiers on opposing teams. Fitness was at the core of his strategy and, also like Roy, he built a family atmosphere at United and became a mentor to many of his players.

But success came at a price for Leeds United. Revie's team was tough and uncompromising, built on gifted but ferocious competitors like Bobby Collins, Johnny Giles, Billy Bremner and Norman Hunter. They were feared by opponents but never loved by anyone but their own fans. Somewhat unfairly, they became known as 'Dirty Leeds', although they did little to dispel the image of an unremitting commitment to winning at all costs. The captain

Billy Bremner even titled his 1969 autobiography *You Get Nowt For Being Second*.

Indeed, the football club was the mirror image of Roy's rugby league Leeds. It was as if football-playing United had adopted the stereotypical hard, dour and unsmiling image of professional rugby league, while Roy's team were the magicians playing Total Rugby League, a beautiful game that left people gasping at its artistry. Whereas Don Revie was secretive and superstitious, Roy was outgoing and scientific. Revie believed the rest of the world was against him, but Roy wanted to win them over with his brand of rugby. Curiously, despite both sides becoming successful at the same time and sharing many common supporters, there was almost no connection between the two clubs, and Roy seems to have only met Don Revie in passing on rare formal occasions.

Although United attracted much bigger crowds, both clubs were aware of each other's success and did not want to be viewed as the city's second team. Roy and the Leeds directors were well-aware that success on the game's only national stage – the Rugby League Challenge Cup Final – was a vital element in their struggle to maintain parity with their round ball neighbours in the south of the city.

In 1967 Roy once again came within 40 minutes of Wembley, when Leeds' Challenge Cup semi-final hopes were extinguished by the eventual cup-winners, Featherstone Rovers. But when the 1967–68 season kicked-off, it seemed like all the pieces that Roy had assembled over the past four years were about to come together.

As autumn turned from October to November Leeds scored 23 tries in just three games. From Christmas, they embarked on a streak of 14 unbeaten league matches, which propelled them once again to finish at the top of the league, seven points ahead of runners-up Wakefield Trinity. In January, when the draw for the first round of the Challenge Cup took place, anticipation and expectation of a trip to Wembley started to stir. In the first three rounds they piled up 65 points and were rewarded with a semi-final against Billy Boston's Wigan.

Roy had a complicated relationship with Wigan. It was the club that had first recognised his talents and brought him north as a 17-year-old. But it was also the club which had sold him to Barrow because of its manager's prejudices. It was the town in which he had lived, married, raised a family, and worked for most of his rugby league career before moving to Hull, but it was also the team which had humiliated him on nationwide television at Wembley in 1960. Now Wigan barred his way to the Twin Towers of the national stadium. Would his Leeds team of youthful talented backs and gnarled forwards finally vanquish his nemesis?

The week before the semi-final, Roy took the squad to watch Wigan play at Salford to study their opponents in detail, something he had never done before. He was determined that the complacency he allowed into Hull's Wembley campaigns would not derail Leeds. 'Roy didn't give us too much to think about, just small stuff and we practised continuously,' said Barry Seabourne. So when the two semi-finalists ran out onto the neutral ground of Swinton in Manchester in front of more than 30,000 fans, Roy was confident his careful preparation would overcome the last obstacle on the road to Wembley.

In team sports, there are rare moments when pressure, fear and nerves evaporate. Time stands still and everything that is desired happens. Passes always go to hand. The ball goes exactly to the right place. Players pop up to support their teammates at precisely the most opportune moment. The sublime becomes the normal, beauty is everywhere, and the result is as natural and as inevitable as the sunrise. And there is nothing that opponents can do about it.

This was one of those golden days. Leeds overwhelmed Wigan 25-4, touching down five times and keeping their own try-line intact. It was a match that all Leeds' players and supporters who were there cherished as perhaps the greatest game in the club's history. 'Every so often in your career there's a match when everything seems to go right and that was the case at Swinton,' recalled left-winger John Atkinson 35 years later. 'Roy must have sat there and thought "this is perfection" and it virtually was. Wigan didn't play badly that day but we just hit an absolute high ... everything that

Roy had been trying came to fruition, it all clicked.' Alan Smith on the right wing felt the same: 'We were all going like a wave, we were just so good on the day. We all did everything he'd ever taught us. Lie deep, move the ball left to right, move them out of position. Everybody seemed to have space that day, and it was only because of that man, Roy Francis.'

Barry Seabourne crowned the day with a darting run from the half-way line, outpacing the Wigan defenders but with five of his own side running alongside him in support as he touched down between the posts. 'Our last try crystallised everything I'd striven for,' said Roy, echoing John Atkinson. 'Perfection on a football field.' As the victorious players left the field, Leeds' fan Mel Rueben remembered how his fellow supporters began chanting Roy's name, in honour of both the victory and its wonderful manner. Once again, Roy was the black leader being acclaimed by his white followers. The love of the Leeds' fans for Roy would be in stark contrast to events exactly two weeks later in Birmingham, when Conservative MP Enoch Powell delivered his notorious 'rivers of blood' speech, in which he predicted that 'the black man will have the whip hand over the white man'.

Now a black leader of white men was on his way to London, to lead his team at the national stadium, Wembley. Leeds' reward for their magnificent semi-final victory was a Cup Final against Wakefield Trinity, their biggest local rivals and arguably the greatest rugby league team of the 1960s. They were also Roy's other bogey team, who had humiliated his Hull side at Wembley in 1960 and defeated his Leeds team in the 1964 Yorkshire Cup Final. Revenge was not a word Roy used, but he had a burning desire to even the account. And, as his players understood, he prized a Wembley victory above all else. 'Roy had this passionate desire to win the Challenge Cup because he had come so close with Hull,' remembered Barry Seabourne.

Unlike Hull's two trips to Wembley, Leeds managed to survive the usual end-of-season fixture congestion unscathed. Roy had learned from the bruising experience of the Hull finals and decided to rest some of his key players, which meant he was able to name a full-strength side for the cup final. On the other hand, Wakefield were without their talisman, the unstoppable try-scoring, goal-kicking centre-three quarter Neil Fox. The winds were blowing in Leeds' favour.

In contrast to his experiences with Hull, Roy's preparation of the team went flawlessly. The team travelled down to London on the Thursday before Cup Final Saturday, and spent Friday morning in a full training session at the Crystal Palace National Sports Centre, London's state-of-the-art athletics training facility. At night the players all went to see a Tom Jones concert at the London Palladium, followed by a trip to the top floor of the Hilton Hotel to enjoy a birds-eye view of the city's night-time skyline. Their wives and girlfriends all travelled down to London in a coach early on the morning of the match. 'Roy made sure we relaxed as much as possible,' recalled Seabourne. To add to their motivation, Leeds chairman Jack Myerscough announced a £100 bonus per player if they won the cup.

Everything was going to plan when Roy and the team arrived at Wembley a couple of hours before the kick-off. There had been bursts of heavy rain on Friday which had left some pools of water on the Wembley pitch but the sun was shining and everyone expected the water to dry off. As they walked around the stadium before getting changed for the match, some of the players chatted to Leeds schoolchildren sitting on the greyhound track at the side of the pitch. It was only when the team was getting changed in the dressing room that they were told there had been a cloudburst and torrential rain was thundering down on the pitch. Conditions could become difficult.

In the last few minutes before kick-off Roy called the dressing room to order. He then went around the room and presented each player with his Wembley jersey. It was a gesture of great emotional significance, tightening the bond between the coach and his players, but also reminding the players that they were now living what for many of them had been their boyhood dream. 'Roy came and gave each one of us our shirt,' John Atkinson told the historian David Hinchliffe 40 years later. 'I filled up with tears when he gave me mine.' As usual, Roy's team talk was short and to the point. Given the weather conditions outside, he wanted his playmakers to kick deep and pull the Wakefield players out of position. Most of all, he wanted them to 'put on a show on a par with the semi-final display against Wigan' recalled Bev Risman. He ended with the words, 'The final act is down to you. You are all prepared, you are all good enough.'

Sadly, no team talk could have prepared the players for the conditions which confronted them during the match. When they came out of the tunnel for the kick-off, the rain had stopped and Wembley was bathed in sunlight. But the pitch was still sodden from the earlier downpour. After an exchange of penalties, John Atkinson slipped trying to pick up a kick from Wakefield's Don Fox, and the ball was pounced on by Ken Hirst, who scored Wakefield's first try. At half-time Leeds were down 7-4.

By the time Atkinson had been awarded a penalty try mid-way through the second half, Wembley looked as if it was being battered by a tropical monsoon, as rain lashed down so hard that parts of the pitch were underwater. With two minutes to go, Barry Seabourne attempted to slice through the Wakefield midfield only to be cut down by a head-high tackle from Harold Poynton. Leeds full-back Bev Risman kicked the resulting penalty from 40 yards out and made the score 11-7 to Leeds. Roy was on the verge of fulfilling his most important ambition.

And then came one of the most extraordinary moments in the history of sport. Wakefield set up to kick-off towards Leeds' right, but at the last moment Don Fox rushed across to kick it to Leeds' left-wing. As the ball skidded and slipped between scrambling Leeds' players, Ken Hirst hacked the ball towards the Leeds' tryline, outpaced six Leeds players, all of whom lost their footing and fell over, and scored a try between the goal-posts. Wakefield were now just one point behind, with a conversion to come that would make them 12-11 winners. The kicker was the ever-reliable Don Fox, who had already been awarded the Lance Todd Trophy by the watching journalists for being the player of the match. Roy, powerless to change the course of events, sat with his head in his hands on the

Leeds bench. 'I just dared not look,' he told *Daily Mirror* reporter Joe Humphreys. His players were dejected as they waited behind the goal. 'That's it, it's gone. We were so deflated,' thought Alan Smith. With the last kick of the match, Fox was about to snatch the Challenge Cup away from Leeds.

But as he kicked the ball, it skidded off his foot and flew outside of the right-hand goalpost. The referee blew the final whistle and Leeds had won the cup. As their fans let out a terrific roar of relief and triumph, Roy lifted his head from his hands. 'I looked up to see John Atkinson, our winger, jumping for joy, then realised the kick must have been missed,' he said 'It meant everything to me. But I feel sorry for Fox, more than any other player I know.' Roy's old friend Eddie Waring felt the same way. 'He's a poor lad, a poor lad,' he exclaimed in his BBC commentary. Many of the Leeds players went to commiserate with Fox as they made their way to the Wembley steps to receive the cup. For many of them, the ecstasy of winning had been undermined by its manner. Some of them even thought that Wakefield had deserved to win. Their glory was the product of an opponent's mistake, not the result of their skills.

No one felt this more than Roy. He had wanted the national stadium to be the stage upon which his side would display its wondrous skills to a nationwide audience. At last, the illegitimate mixed-race boy who had risked everything to leave Wales to try and succeed in the hard world of professional sport, who had fought for and won respect, and even love, in working-class towns across northern England, would be acknowledged in the nation's stadium. But on the greatest day of his sporting career he had won by mere chance. He 'felt his team had been denied the chance to show what it was truly capable of,' wrote Bev Risman later.

What should have been an evening of joyous celebration turned out to be a dispiriting anti-climax. Roy took the players for a congratulatory drink in one of the bars at the Hilton Hotel but they felt out of place among the well-heeled guests of the prestigious hotel. As two dozen working-class northerners led by a black man entered the hotel, 'You could see people looking, thinking, "Who's this load of vagabonds coming in here?"' recalled

John Atkinson. They soon left and went on to the Park Lane Hotel for the official team celebration gala dinner. But Roy didn't go to the dinner. He and Rene went back to their hotel room and ate alone. Disappointment is not a dish that can easily be shared.

For 32 years, as a player and a coach, Roy had striven to win rugby league's most glittering prize. Now the Challenge Cup was his, but the glory was not.

8

Black Leader in White Australia: 1968–1971

'I'm no Messiah.'

If the taste of Wembley victory had not been as sweet as Roy had hoped, the first few weeks of the 1968–69 season brought him a rising sense of satisfaction.

As Leeds swept all before them, it was clear that a dynasty had been born. 'I have seen all the Leeds teams since 1919,' confessed the *Yorkshire Post's* Leslie Tremlett, 'but I have never seen a Leeds side surpass in team-work the existing one. I do not think I have seen a Leeds one equal to it.' In the opening friendly match of the season against local rivals Hunslet, 16-year-old John Holmes, earmarked as the future replacement for Bev Risman at full-back, kicked 10 goals and scored a try. Other than the 30-year-old Risman, all of Leeds' Wembley backline were in their early 20s and their youthful talent and enthusiasm soon began to flourish. Apart from two early losses, Leeds went unbeaten in the league until their very last match. And in the first knock-out completion of the season, the Yorkshire Cup, they brushed aside their opponents in an unstoppable march to the final.

There, marshalled by the 21-year-old scrum-half Barry Seabourne, Leeds comprehensively defeated Castleford to lift the trophy for the first time in a decade. For Roy, it was his first Yorkshire Cup victory in six final appearances, and it meant he had now won every available rugby league trophy. And, unlike Wembley, Leeds had won in the style Roy wanted. A true celebration could now be held and the team travelled back to Headingley to a party in the Leeds supporters club bar.

As the party drew to a close, Roy stood up to thank the players and the fans, and announced that, as captain Mick Clark would be retiring at the end of the season, he was making Barry Seabourne the new Leeds captain, the club's youngest ever. The bar erupted in cheers. He had not told the modest Seabourne of his appointment, who was perhaps more surprised than anyone else in the room. It was Roy at his most charismatic, rewarding one of his favourite players with a grand gesture, and commanding the audience with his authority and generosity. Barry was to be Roy's new Johnny Whiteley, the inspirational fulcrum around which the Leeds dynasty was to be built.

But just 10 days later, the Leeds directors agreed to release Roy from his contract. Eleven days after that, he coached his last game for the club. Roy Francis' Leeds would no longer be Roy's team.

FAREWELL TO A DYNASTY

Roy's relationship with the Leeds board had been strained for some months. When he joined the club in October 1963 he signed a contract up to the summer of 1967. He then signed a one-year extension which took him up to the summer of 1968. With the team firmly on top of the league table and a Wembley appearance in the offing, Roy expected to be rewarded with a long-term contract. After all, he had achieved everything he said he would, and his young team was expected to dominate the sport for years to come. In Roy's eyes, a five-year contract seemed to be both fair and justifiable.

But despite his achievements, the Leeds board would not make such a commitment. In the days after the Wembley victory, the tensions between Roy and the board spilled out and became apparent to the players. Alan Smith remembered overhearing a heated argument between Roy and Leeds' managing director Alf Rutherford one day at Headingley: 'Roy wanted a new contract and we were all aware that Roy wasn't happy after the Wembley win.' It wasn't the first time they'd clashed; at one point Rutherford refused permission for the Leeds players to train on the Headingley pitch, an order which Roy simply ignored. Twenty years later, Roy recalled ruefully his frustration with the club: 'All I wanted from the Leeds board was a sign they wanted to retain my services, not necessarily greater financial reward, but a sense of feeling appreciated.'

To some extent he perhaps became a victim of his own success. He had transformed Leeds into one of the leading, and most attractive, teams in the sport. The directors had now got what they wanted and saw no reason to give him the increased power over the club that a long-term contract would bring. The traditional view of the directors – 'we are the masters here' – was one they upheld vigorously. In their eyes, they were the club and no one could be bigger than them.

The colour of Roy's skin also seems to have been a factor. The idea of a black man being an authority figure was still unacceptable to many sections of British society, and Roy told his son Geoff that he felt this had influenced how he was treated. Geoff's wife Anne, who regularly went to matches with Rene during the 1960s, also remembered that, 'Roy always thought that there was a lot of prejudice there.' Indeed, the Leeds board did not have a good track record on racial issues. Despite enjoying huge support from the city's large Jewish community, it was an open secret that the directors would not allow a Jewish person to join the board. As the number of Leeds' wealthy Jewish businessmen increased in the post-war period, many of them felt frustrated by the unspoken anti-Semitism of their club's officials and turned their attention to Leeds United, so beginning a long history of prominent Jewish directors of the soccer club.

Discussions about a new contract were put on hold in June 1968 when Roy flew out to Sydney for a six-week stint as a coaching consultant to the North Sydney Bears rugby league club. The Bears had been a chronically underachieving club, winning only two Premierships (as the Australians called their league championships) in 60 years of its existence, and over the last decade had reached the premiership play-offs just twice. The Bears' chairman Harry McKinnon was determined to change its dismal history. He had become friendly with the former Hull full-back Colin Hutton when Hutton coached Great Britain on the 1962 tour to Australia, and the two stayed in touch. When McKinnon asked Hutton for advice about a new coach, Hutton recommended his mentor Roy Francis. A connection was made and Roy agreed to a six-week coaching consultancy at the Bears at the end of Leeds' season.

It did not begin well. When Roy walked through the arrivals gate at Sydney's Mascot Airport, Harry McKinnon didn't recognise him at first because he didn't realise that Roy was black. Roy didn't take offence and there was no repeat of the Pin Macmillan affair at Manchester airport in 1957. Indeed, Norths already had the Indigenous Australians George Ambrum and Eric Pitt playing for them. A greater problem was that they had appointed Roy without consulting the current coach, Col Greenwood, who was deeply offended, and the players threatened to go on strike in support of him. The situation was compounded because Greenwood was a white South African who had played for the Springboks before switching codes to join Wakefield Trinity and, as he made clear to the historian Andrew Moore in 1995, was a supporter of the apartheid regime. However, Greenwood dissuaded the team from going on strike, and instead took legal action against the club. He also wrote a personal letter to Roy, wishing him the best of luck at Norths.

Once Roy arrived at the club, the controversy evaporated and his six weeks at North Sydney turned out to be very successful. Under Greenwood, the Bears had won only one of their first 12 matches of the season, but Roy steered them to three wins in the six games he was there. He quickly diagnosed the team's losing mentality as one of its biggest barriers to success. 'He is working on the players' minds as well as on the condition of their bodies,' reported Sydney's weekly *Rugby League News*. 'He believes that much of Norths' trouble is mental – he is trying to have them realise that they are as good as the next man.' He was hailed as the club's saviour, and the *Rugby League News* named him as one of its 'Five Personalities of 68' on the basis of just six matches. His leadership galvanised the whole team, as Brian Norton, a popular North Sydney forward who would later also coach the club, recalled: 'In those six weeks, Roy made a huge impression on not only the players, but also the whole district of North Sydney. Everyone was excited because the following year we were going to have a coach that would take North Sydney to a premiership.'

When Roy returned to England at the start of August 1968, he seemed to have the best of both worlds. By going to the Bears he had put pressure on Leeds to give him the contract he felt he deserved, and he now had the option to return to Sydney and conquer a new world. In reality, he had given himself no room for manoeuvre. The Leeds directors were experienced businessmen who were used to dealing with recalcitrant employees. They called his bluff and offered him just a two-year contract extension. Roy was now forced to choose between accepting an unsatisfactory deal or emigrating to Australia.

For a man as proud as Roy, he could not lose face by accepting a contract he felt was disrespectful. But the Leeds directors refused to budge. On the other hand, Roy wanted to go to Australia on his own terms, and did not want to accept Norths' offer just because he was backed into a corner. When the contract from Sydney arrived, his son Ian remembers him saying: '"You know what? I'm going to put some demands in here to see if they really want me." Because he always wanted to know if people really wanted him for himself. So he asked for flights back home via Fiji and the Caribbean at the end of every season, and for double the wages. And Norths just wrote back and said yes.'

His North Sydney contract was finalised at ten thousand Australian dollars a year for three years plus bonuses and expenses, making him in the words of *Rugby League News*, 'The highest paid personality in rugby league'. He formally asked Leeds to release him from his contract on 17 September and told reporters that 'subject to the contract being signed and, of course, my release from Leeds, I have decided to accept the offer made to me by the North Sydney club'. Eventually after six weeks, the Leeds directors agreed to his request to be released. His last match in charge of his team was on a wintry Saturday afternoon in York on 9 November when, in tribute to Roy's style of rugby, his players ran in seven tries in a 39-8 victory.

There was one last act before he and Rene left for Sydney. A farewell party was held at the Leeds Supporters' Club at Headingley, where both were presented with gifts in appreciation of the success they had brought the club and the community they had created. Lifelong Leeds fan Mel Reuben spoke for thousands when he looked back and said, 'We loved Roy. We loved the way he played. We loved going to watch the team.' Those same sentiments were also shared by thousands of rugby league fans in Hull. Would they also come to be shared by supporters of the North Sydney Bears?

HEADING NORTH DOWN UNDER

On the face of it, the common bond of rugby league linking the north of England to Australia's eastern states of Queensland and New South Wales would indicate that Roy would be successful again. The sport had emerged Down Under in 1907 when, just as in England, rugby had been ripped in two over the issue of whether working-class players should be compensated for playing the game.

The tensions between the sport's patrician leaders and the industrial workers who made up the majority of Australian rugby players and spectators were symbolised by the case of Alec Burdon. He was injured playing rugby union for New South Wales against Queensland in 1907 and not only lost wages because he could not work but also had to pay his own medical expenses. Anger at this manifest unfairness simmered so strongly that when the first-ever New Zealand rugby league team arrived in Sydney in August that year, tensions reached boiling point and rugby fractured along class lines. The first rugby league club season began in 1908 and within five years, league had overtaken union as the dominant sport of

New South Wales and Queensland. As in northern England, league was a game of the industrial working classes, as could be seen on the pitch, in the grandstands and by the large number of Labour Party and trade union officials who also administered the new game.

North Sydney was one of the league's founding clubs and had won back-to-back premierships in 1921 and 1922. But a year later, work started on the construction of the Harbour Bridge, which was to link Sydney's North with the rest of the city. This led to the destruction of many hundreds of working-class homes in the North Sydney district, and by the time the bridge opened in 1932, local demographics had changed considerably. What was once a community of dockers, ferry workers and other industrial trades now became the home for many of Sydney's professional classes. Although the effects weren't immediate, Norths struggled to attract fans and players as the area became gentrified. The 1966 construction of the huge Warringah Expressway also ripped out much of the heart of the district. Eventually, the years of failure took its toll, and the club became used to losing. When Ken Irvine, arguably its greatest ever player, resigned from the club committee in 1975 he declared he was 'just fed up with the whole unprofessional attitude of North Sydney'.

In stark contrast to today's highly commercialised National Rugby League, rugby league in Australia until the 1980s was organised on a part-time, unprofessional basis. Clubs were dominated by secretaries and committeemen whose priorities were to guard their privileges and status in the networks of 'mates' who ran the game. One of those networks was Sydney's tabloid journalists, whose intense scrutiny orchestrated a daily soap opera of gossip, intrigue and factionalism. They not only sold newspapers but also often set the agenda for rugby league's administrators. Not even in English soccer did the press play such a central role in the day-to-day life of a sport.

In the 1960s, Sydney rugby league had begun to change, in large part due to the legalisation of poker machines, otherwise known in Britain as 'one-armed bandits'. 'Leagues clubs', the social clubs attached to rugby league teams, grew rich thanks to the ease with which casual, and the not-so-casual, gamblers could pour money into the slots of the machines. The leagues clubs passed this money back to their league team, who often spent it on signing up top British players. By the time that Roy arrived back in Sydney in 1969, stars like St Helens' Dick Huddart and Wigan's Dave Bolton were as well known in Sydney as they were in England. As Roy would find out, these players discovered a game in Australia which was very similar to that in England, but also very different.

How much Roy realised this when he and Rene set sail for Sydney is open to question. His six-week stint with North Sydney in 1968 had been a whirlwind visit during which he was feted and praised but given little time to fathom the complexities of this new world. The old certainties around which he had built his career and life were not so sure anymore.

One of the clauses Roy had inserted into his contract with Norths specified that the club would pay for a first-class cabin on the SS *Canberra* to take him and Rene on the five-week voyage to Australia. Launched in 1960 by P&O Lines, the *Canberra* was the biggest British-built ocean liner for 30 years, equipped with the most luxurious cabins of any British passenger ship. The Hollywood star Cary Grant famously sailed on her in 1967, underlining the glamour and opulence which ocean liners still symbolised even as long-haul air travel began to eat into their market. The *Canberra* emphasised the common bond between Britain and Australia by featuring portraits of famous cricketers among the many artworks which adorned its corridors. But if Roy felt reassured when he saw the portrait of the great West Indian cricketer Learie Constantine, it was a feeling which would not last.

As the *Canberra* arrived at Cape Town and the passengers were preparing to disembark to go sight-seeing, Roy was informed that he would not be allowed to get off the ship while it was docked in South Africa. The country's apartheid laws did not allow non-white people to go into areas which had been designated for whites. The strict division of the races by South Africa's apartheid government meant that Roy was not allowed to be a tourist like his fellow passengers. Moreover, he and Rene would not even have been able to hold hands if they set foot on South African soil. Inter-racial relationships were illegal and their marriage was a criminal offence under apartheid law.

The couple endured this indignity with stoicism, but the humiliation must have cut deep. After decades of creating an environment where he could protect himself and his family from the dehumanising impacts of racism, he was now powerless in the face of apartheid. Roy Francis may have been one of the *Canberra*'s first-class passengers and arguably the world's foremost rugby coach, but to South Africa's apartheid regime he was just another black man to be kept in his segregated place.

When they finally arrived in Australia on 3 February, 1969, things could not have seemed more different. Roy's arrival was enthusiastically reported in all of the Sydney newspapers and a couple of days later, photographers assembled at North Sydney to record the new coach's first meeting with his team. 'I expect a lot from you,' he told the players as he announced a new four-days-a-week training schedule, 'but I know you can do it. Everything is up to you. There's no easy road for a football team these days.' He ends with a typical rhetorical flourish: 'If there's anyone here that's not interested in playing football, please let me know.'

No one did, and the Bears' first match of 1969 saw them travel to Parramatta and run away with a six-try 28-18 victory. 'Francis Magic inspires Norths' proclaimed the widely-respected journalist Alan Clarkson, although Roy presciently warned the press, 'I'm no Messiah.' When the league competition kicked off, the Bears ran in 69 points in an unbeaten first three matches, which took them to the top of the table. It wasn't to last. The team became frustratingly inconsistent despite playing attractive attacking rugby. Roy was not surprised because he was well aware that the rebuilding of Norths was a long-term project.

As at Hull and Leeds, he set about building a family culture at his new club. One of his first initiatives would have perhaps been unthinkable for any other coach: he and Rene offered to babysit for players and their wives if they wanted to attend club functions. 'Our idea in making the baby-sitting offer was to

encourage players' wives not to resent the time football demands
from their husbands,' he told *Rugby League World*. This was a new
twist on his 'happy wife, happy life' philosophy but it worked.
The club provided the couple with a large house five minutes'
walk from Norths' picturesque ground, and it soon became
a gathering place for players and their families. 'On Saturday
mornings the day before the game he would always bring four
or five players round and cook them steaks. He was building
up team spirit,' remembered Jim Mills, who arrived at the club
from Bradford Northern in 1970. 'People enjoyed going round
to their house. They thought, "The team is our family." And they
treated you like you were part of their family.' Rene became very
popular in the club and was dubbed 'Big Red' by the players and
their wives because of her red hair and height. For Jim Mills,
'She was like my mother when I was there. She always had a
smile for you, even if Roy wasn't happy with you. She always
made you feel at home.'

In April 1969 Roy signed Graham Williams, a scheming, tricky
scrum-half who had starred for Swinton in England. Not dissimilar
to Barry Seabourne in Roy's Leeds team, Williams was an organiser
and playmaker who brought direction and tactical nous to the
Bears. He was just what the team needed, and initially made a
huge difference to the side. But his impact was undermined by the
large number of penalties he conceded during matches. Australian
referees' interpretations of rugby league rules sometimes differed
in small ways from England, especially in the scrum, but Roy also
suspected there was an 'anti-Pommie' bias against English players.

Whatever the reason, by June the penalty count against Williams
had become a liability and Roy dropped him from the team. He
returned for the next match but at stand-off half rather than his
usual scrum-half position. Away from the scrum, Williams was
less likely to be penalised but was not playing in his best position.
This upset the team's equilibrium and for the rest of the season
Norths remained frustratingly close to, but outside of, the play-off
places. The bright promise that opened the campaign ended in a
dull seventh place in the league.

The season was also soured for Roy because he found that criticism of him in the Sydney press often highlighted his race. Terry Smith of the *Daily Mirror* accused him of acting 'like an authoritarian witch doctor' who had 'cast a spell over the North Sydney players,' while the *Daily Telegraph*'s Mike Gibson described him as a 'dark gentleman'. Jim Mills remembered that one journalist would call the team 'Roy Francis and his North Sydney black and white minstrels'. For someone who had spent a lifetime shielding himself from such insults, the press focus on his colour became increasingly stressful. No doubt he hoped that a successful season at North Sydney would force them to focus on his achievements instead.

THE SEASON IN HELL

In October 1969, a few weeks into the Australian off-season, Roy and Rene flew back to England for three months. He met with Bradford Northern officials to set up a scholarship scheme to send young Norths' players to Bradford Northern to gain experience, and talked to a number of players about moving to Sydney to play under him. Feeling that Norths' forwards lacked steel, he spoke to Jim Mills, the big, fiery Welsh prop-forward who was then playing for Bradford. Mills, whose terrifying on-field presence was equalled only by his warm and generous personality off it, had been told informally that he would be selected for the 1970 Great Britain tour to Australia. However, Roy's charm persuaded him otherwise: '"Listen," he said, "come out to Australia to play for North Sydney and I'll get you a good contract." I said, "But I'm on the tour" and Roy said, "You can always go on tour." He talked me into it at the bar! I didn't have much money at the time so he arranged to get me a couple of thousand quid in cash. And off I went to Australia.'

So when the new Australian season kicked off on 28 March, 1970, Roy's rebuilding plan seemed to be taking shape. Not only had he signed one of Britain's best forwards, he had also appointed a new captain in Ken Irvine, the idol of Norths' supporters and a truly great winger, and introduced a modern new playing strip of all-white with a band of red and black, the club's traditional colours. Optimism surged.

It lasted just 39 minutes. In the first match of the season at Canterbury-Bankstown, Irvine was fouled as he dived on a loose ball close to Norths' try-line. An all-in brawl broke out which resulted in Norths' vice-captain John McDonnell being sent off by referee Keith Page. When Irvine asked the referee why no Canterbury players had even been cautioned, Page also sent him off for using abusive language. Enraged by this apparent injustice, Irvine told his players to leave the field. As a number started to follow him, they were met on the sideline by panicked Norths officials, including Roy, who told them to get back on the pitch and play. Tempers cooled at half-time and the 11-player Norths actually led until the last couple of minutes of the match when a converted try won the game for Canterbury.

The walk-off made it to prime-time TV news and the front pages of the dailies, and fed the Sydney media's insatiable appetite for rugby league news for days on end. The investigation by the rugby league authorities lasted a fortnight and resulted in Ken Irvine being given a one match ban for the sending-off and a further two for inciting the walk-off. Even worse, the club came out of the affair looking foolish and disorganised, a throw-back to its bad old days.

It was the opposite of everything Roy had worked for. He had always prided himself on his teams' refusal to be provoked and to remain disciplined. To argue with the referee was not something a Roy Francis team ever did. What's more, he had put his personal trust in Ken Irvine. For Roy, the captain was his representative on the pitch, as had been Johnny Whiteley at Hull and Barry Seabourne at Leeds, and he expected him to behave honourably. Irvine's actions were unacceptable and marked the start of a breakdown in relations between the two men which brought serious ramifications for both of them.

Things then went from bad to worse. Just four days after the conclusion of the walk-off investigation, Norths were ripped apart 40-20 at home to St George. They had now lost all four of their opening matches and conceded 111 points. Roy had reached breaking point. He stormed into the Norths dressing room, lifted up his shirt and pointed to his skin. 'To be born with this is to be born with humiliation,' he shouted at the players, 'but I was not born with this humiliation,' he added as he looked them in the eye. It was an extraordinary statement, a flash of rage against players he felt had embarrassed and betrayed him, but also an instantaneous rush to the surface of suppressed frustrations which had been building up since coming to Sydney.

The febrile Sydney press sensed blood. Rather than offering sympathy or asking what was behind Roy's expression of anger, reporters double-downed on his skin colour. 'As an exercise in method acting, the performance has already been compared with Sir Laurence Olivier's Othello,' declared *Rugby League Week*, 'but many were of the opinion that it carried a dash of Malcolm X.' Of course, no one asked why skin colour was causing Roy to feel humiliation.

The sluice gates of personal criticism were now well and truly open. Although Roy told the post-match press conference that he would see out his contract at Norths, the *Sydney Morning Herald* reported that he said he would leave at the end of the following year. Norths were tipped to finish bottom of the league, despite being only four weeks into the season, and questions were asked about Roy's salary and expenses. Some committee members were not happy with him controlling team selection and player recruitment, which they saw as their prerogative, and leaked stories to the press about the amount of money he was spending. Norm Strong, a former captain and committee member, complained that Roy's half-time talks weren't rousing enough, but that had never been his style. 'He would give observations at half-time but never got angry,' explained Leeds' Drew Broatch. 'He was very constructive but he expected the most from his players. There was no need for him to bollock players.'

Eventually Roy steadied the ship and Norths won their first match in six attempts on 2 May, but it was an unpleasant and bumpy ride to the end of the season. The club eventually finished

ninth out of 12 teams, a mediocre season typical of Norths before
Roy's appointment. By then his relationship with Ken Irvine had
completely collapsed because, as Jim Mills saw, Irvine 'didn't like
Roy's discipline. He was keen on drinking and Roy found out and
that was it. But he was a legend at Norths and Roy didn't really
think it through. When he got rid of Ken the crowd didn't like it.'
Although Roy liked a drink himself, his attitude to players drinking
during the season – 'a fit footballer's need for alcohol should be
very low and taken at the right time' – had little in common with
the regular drinking to excess that was commonplace in Sydney
rugby league.

    In truth, Norths had expected Roy to create a Premiership-
winning side in a couple of seasons, but he had never been a
get-rich-quick coach. At Hull and Leeds it had taken him five
seasons to create the team he wanted. 'They were over-ambitious
and didn't have the patience,' he reflected in 1986. When success
didn't come overnight, Norths' laid-back traditions meant that
many players and officials felt the sacrifice and discipline required
to win consistently were not worth falling out about. The club
simply lacked the professionalism which Roy expected from his
teams. Roy Masters, the Sydney rugby league coach and newspaper
columnist, agreed with former Norths coach Noel Kelly, who
told him that the club's lack of success was down to 'too many
good blokes'. Dennis Cubis, one of the players at the centre of
the walk-off controversy, reflected in the 1990s that, 'I don't think
Roy managed to continue with the promise he initially showed. I
don't think that eventually he managed to draw the response in the
players which he initially managed to achieve.'

    Even the loyal Jim Mills felt a twinge of disillusionment when
the Great Britain Lions arrived in June 1970 and won the rugby
league Ashes against Australia. 'I was stood on the terraces watching
the Third Test and I thought, I could have been on there,' he said.
He had come to regret that he didn't go on the tour. 'Roy wanted
me to sign but the advice he gave wasn't really the best advice – it
was from his point of view because he wanted a big prop.' The
final note of disillusion came from the man who had recruited Roy,

Norths' chairman Harry McKinnon, who limply told the club's annual general meeting in December, 'Whether we like it or not, he is here for another 12 months. I would suggest that we get behind him and support him.'

Poor performances on the field and endless controversies off it took a tremendous toll on Roy. It culminated in him walking out of a live broadcast of the *Saturday World of Sport*, a sports panel show on Sydney's Channel 9 hosted by the self-styled controversialist Ron Casey, an early right-wing shock-jock who became notorious for his comments about Aboriginal Australians, Asians, Jews, women, and pretty much everyone else who he didn't consider a fair dinkum white Aussie bloke. Casey had been a thorn in Roy's side throughout the season and his provocative needling of him during the programme made Roy feel, in the words of journalist Mike Gibson, 'That Casey was discriminating against him and making references to his colour.' The show was later satirised by the playwright Alex Buzo in his thinly disguised 1971 play *The Roy Murphy Show*, in which a fictionalised Roy Francis appeared as coach Samuel Bow, who walks off the show after enduring insults from the host. For Roy, the Casey interview was the lowest point of the disrespect and race-baiting he had endured from the Sydney media. Perhaps worst of all for him, following his venting of rage after Norths' humiliation against St George, was that this was now the second time he had allowed his anger to get the better of him, revealing his emotions and undermining the self-assured image he projected to the world.

The events of 1970 seem to have sent him into a downward spiral towards depression. When the Great Britain touring team came to Sydney in early June, Johnny Whiteley, now a successful coach in his own right who was masterminding the Lions' campaign for the Ashes, went to see his old mentor. 'He wasn't getting on well,' he said. 'He was sort of self-isolating and became a recluse. I went and had a day with him at his house. He was still going to the club but it was club-home, home-club.' Jim Mills, who was lodging in the house next door to Roy and Rene, had the same worries: 'They never went out, him and Rene. They just sat in the house and never went anywhere. The only people they saw were players. I remember thinking, it's not much of a life for her. Roy only ever went for a drink after the match.'

One of the reasons for not leaving the house was to avoid the casual racism from which Roy had largely insulated himself in England. But that was far more difficult in Australia, and not simply because its rugby league press was much more intrusive. Australia had only started to change the overtly racist laws of its 'White Australia' era in the mid-1960s, as Aboriginal people fought for civil rights and the government tried to modernise the image of the country. When Charlie Williams accepted a contract to play for the Australian soccer club Auburn in 1962 he was refused a visa by the Australian Embassy because he was not white. It was not until 1967 that Aboriginal people were counted in the national census or that non-European immigrants were given equal rights to citizenship. The famous 'Ten Pound Pom' assisted passage to Australia scheme which saw a million Britons emigrate Down Under between 1945 and 1982 remained a 'whites-only' policy until the 1970s.

Roy and Rene were a high-profile interracial couple in a society where laws had slowly started to change but attitudes lagged far behind. They could not have failed to experience the everyday racism of Australian society. Roland Davis, who had watched Roy play in the 1940s and was working in Sydney in the late 1960s, was shocked at how commonplace racism was: 'I couldn't believe how the nice people I was working with talked about Aboriginal people like that. I can remember when we moved to Brisbane and I took my son to the tennis to watch Evonne Goolagong, who had just won Wimbledon. I couldn't believe the lukewarm reception she got from the crowd.' When Roy and Rene returned home to England for Christmas in 1970, they remarked how the Australian press talked about 'Roy's Minstrels' and 'Roy X'.

When they flew back to Australia in January 1971, Roy fully intended to stay until his contract ended in September. But even before the new season had begun, he was confronted with further challenges. At the start of February, Ken Irvine was transferred to

Manly, ending his deadlocked relationship with Roy but unleashing a wave of criticism from Norths' fans who had lost the club's favourite son to its bitterest rival. From being the messiah, Roy was now a villain. A fortnight later, Graham Williams' wife Patricia was killed during a parachute jump for charity when she accidentally landed in a dam and drowned. In a stark contrast to the fatherly figure he had always previously been for his players, Roy didn't accompany Williams to identify his wife's body but asked Jim Mills to go in his place. It seems the emotional toll of the previous 18 months had drained Roy of the capacity to deal with the tragedy.

A few days later Rene called her sons in England and told them: 'I'm bringing him home. They are crucifying him and he's going to have a nervous breakdown.' On 10 March, two weeks before the new season began, Roy told the North Sydney committee that he was resigning. 'I am leaving Norths because I have bought a pub in England,' he told Ray Chesterton of the *Sydney Sun*. 'I have put two of my other businesses on the market to help raise funds to redecorate it.' He had to return now in order to make sure the pub was refurbished in time for the busy summer holiday season. On behalf of Norths, Harry McKinnon likened his outgoing coach to 'a great artist, who possibly never achieved much in his time, but when he passed on, his work became famous'.

A few weeks later, he and Rene were gone. Their overwhelming desire to leave Australia was captured by a classified advertisement that appeared at the end of March in the *Sydney Morning Herald* for a Holden Premier 186 car, 'The property of Mr Roy Francis who is returning to the UK and wishes a quick sale'.

WHO CRUCIFIED ROY?

In some respects Roy had been a victim of the culture of the North Sydney club. They expected too much of him in too short a time, and were unable to respond to his demands for professional attitudes. But nor could Roy deal with the intense backroom politics of the Sydney rugby league clubs. He assumed that, as in England, control of team affairs meant just that, and did not appreciate the tenacity of the 'mates' culture of the club in protecting what committeemen saw as their rights and privileges.

There were a few Norths players who understood what Roy was trying to do. Veteran hooker Ross Warner thought he 'was probably the finest coach I ever met. I think he was about 10 years in front of anybody.' Brian Norton also lamented his going: 'I still believe that if Norths had let stability take its course, if they'd have let Francis stay for another three or four years, I believe he would have got them the premiership.' But it was an almost impossible task, and no one who followed Roy as Norths' coach ever succeeded. The club would never reach a premiership grand final before it was forced to drop down into the second tier of Sydney rugby league in 1999.

The culture of Norths and its backroom politics was only one part of the problem. The main challenge which confronted Roy was racism. It doesn't appear to have been an issue at the club itself; he never criticised them for racist attitudes, and he and Rene continued to entertain players at their home until they left. But beyond the club, racism from the media and society itself bore down heavily on Roy. The endless references to skin colour and the supposed exoticism of Roy coaching Norths ground him down, constantly reminding him he was being judged for something other than his coaching ability. 'The main thing that caused me to leave was the vilification of some of the press,' he told the journalist Neil Cadigan in 1986. Unlike in Hull and Leeds, where he had the complete trust of his players, he could not build a family bubble of players and their wives as his shield against the daily injustices of the world. The American writer James Baldwin once wrote how he learned as a young man that to be black 'meant precisely that one was never looked at, but was simply at the mercy of the reflexes the colour of one's skin caused in other people'. In Australia Roy was confronted by the same truth. No matter what his experience or expertise, his colour defined how he was seen by the media.

From being a father figure and a mentor to his teams, Roy had become merely one more tall poppy that Sydney's media was waiting to cut down to size. Although hard for many in rugby league to accept, it was racism that forced Roy Francis out of Australia, as one Sydney journalist admitted shortly after Roy announced his departure: 'When all of your critics are through dealing with you, Mr Francis, Sydney will be only too willing to forget you. Unfortunate but true. You are coloured, you see, Mr Francis, and even if you were the reincarnation of Dally Messenger, you would not have made it in the small world that is Sydney Rugby League.'

9

The Hard Road from the Top: 1971–1989

'Rugby that brought not only entertainment and success, but also respect.'

Roy and Rene left Sydney on 13 April, 1971, never to return to Australia. They sailed across the Pacific and the Atlantic and arrived back home in May. Roy immediately threw himself into the refurbishment of the pub he had bought, the Buckles Inn, midway on the main road from Leeds to York.

The Buckles mirrored the changing times. It had been built in 1938 as a modern 'roadhouse' pub to attract the growing numbers of car drivers and provide them with meals and other refreshments. A pub had been on the site since Georgian times and the name derived from Ann Buckles, the landlady in the 1840s and 1850s. By the time Roy took over, roadhouse pubs were being transformed into family eating establishments, well-known for dishes such as prawn cocktail and chicken in a basket. No longer an expensive luxury, there were now over 13 million private cars in Britain and the idea of driving out to a pub for a meal in the evening or at the weekend had become highly fashionable.

During the war, Roy had been based near the Buckles at Askham Bryan military camp. In later years he often drove past the pub, imagining it to be the perfect business opportunity. Now that he had been able to take over, he set about converting it into a stylish and modern restaurant-pub. He still owned cafes in Leeds but the Buckles was a significant step up. He decided he wanted the pub's interior to be based on an American-style diner, so he dispatched Geoff and Ian on a 10-day trip to America to bring back the best ideas from diners and restaurants there. His vision brought him into conflict with the controlling brewery, who wanted to retain the traditional image of the pub.

Never one to back down in an argument, Roy eventually prevailed and the newly-refurbished Buckles opened for business in December 1971. The opening night was attended by England cricketers Brian Close and Fred Trueman, comedian Norman Collier, former Great Britain captain Jeff Stevenson, and Johnny Whiteley, Tommy Harris and Frankie Broadhurst from Hull's glory years. Guests wore formal evening wear and the champagne flowed. Roy and Rene each gave a little speech, with Rene calculating that the Buckles was her 31st move since she married Roy and that she had 'decided to stay put and not move again'. As she probably knew as soon as the words came out of her mouth, this was not to be.

Just eight weeks after the Buckles' gala opening, the *Hull Daily Mail* suggested 'Roy's vast experience could do some club a power of good' and that he might be 'hankering to get back in the game in some capacity'. Although it might have been only newspaper speculation, Roy was so well-connected among rugby league journalists it is unlikely he had nothing to do with the story. He had certainly kept informal contacts with clubs. In November 1970, shortly after returning to England from Australia for a Christmas break, he had met Hull FC chairman Charles Watson at the Rugby League World Cup Final at Headingley. 'When you finish in Australia, you can come back to the Boulevard,' Watson joked with him, unaware that Roy would actually be finishing at North Sydney just three months later.

In fact, Watson was only half-joking. The years since Roy left Hull had not been kind to the club. Despite the coaching of Johnny Whiteley and the world-class brilliance of Clive Sullivan, the team had never been more than middling. It had not finished higher than ninth in the league, and its trophy cabinet would have been bare but for a single Yorkshire Cup Final win in 1969. 'The good players were getting old and the new ones weren't really good enough,' remembered Keith Tindall, who played his first game for the club in January 1972. Even worse, their crosstown rivals Hull KR had consistently finished higher in the league every season since Roy's departure. Hull's decline led to a succession of factional disputes and boardroom coups. By 1972, average crowds at the Boulevard had dropped to less than two thousand, a pitiful fraction of the five-figure attendances which crammed in during Roy's reign. This decline took place in the midst of growing economic problems for the city, where unemployment reached its highest level since 1939 and was almost double the national rate.

Something had to be done to revive the club. When the 1971–72 season finished, the board of directors decided to sack the current coach Ivor Watts, the club's stalwart winger of the 1940s and 1950s. But Watts had been in the game long enough to know what was planned for him, so when he was called into the boardroom to discuss his fate, he preempted the directors by handing them his resignation. Peter Charlesworth, a solicitor and lifelong Hull fan whose grandfather and father had also been club officials, had just been appointed to the board when this drama broke out. 'Johnny Whiteley offered to come back as interim coach if he could pick the team,' he remembered. 'But the nine-man board picked the team and was reluctant to let go of its power. So Johnny then said, why don't you talk to Roy because he's back from Australia? Roy took some persuading because he was living in Leeds and didn't agree at once. He wasn't that keen but we persuaded him.'

On the Saturday night of 6 May, 1972, the local *Sports Mail* triumphantly announced 'Roy Francis is back in Hull as Team Boss' on its front page. 'This is a major step to put the club back among the rugby league elite,' Charles Watson declared excitedly. Hull fans everywhere walked a little more proudly and expectantly when they heard the news. Roy said he would be taking up his duties later in June but persuaded Ivor Watts to stay on as an assistant coach and start pre-season training with the players.

Two weeks later, Roy asked Johnny Whiteley to join as another assistant. 'When he came back, I thought, here we go again!' recalled Johnny.

But you can't swim in the same river twice, and it soon became clear that Roy was reluctant to commit himself fully to coaching. On 10 August, 10 days before the new season kicked-off, the club announced it had given him a month's leave of absence to look after Rene, who had become 'indisposed' managing their businesses while Roy was coaching in Hull. This was true: Roy had essentially left the running of the Buckles in Rene's hands, a role she neither wanted nor enjoyed.

Roy's stepping back from coaching duties may also have been caused by what he had seen of the state of the club. The directors were still reluctant to spend money on buying players from outside of the city, the Boulevard stadium was crumbling, and an air of directionless dilapidation hung over the club. He was not impressed, telling the directors that 'money has to be found because the team lacks strength in depth, which only leads to complacency among the players. ... We must not penny-pinch. We have to attack this with determination and foresight'.

It was to no avail. The club was paralysed by endless subterranean battles for control between rival shareholder groups. This came to a head just three days into the season. Chairman Charles Watson opened the club's annual general meeting, describing how Roy was turning things around and that the club could now look forward confidently. Thirty minutes later, Watson had been voted off the board, the deputy chairman had resigned in protest, and a new chairman, Charles Clegg, installed. For Roy, the brutal ousting of Watson was one more dispiriting aspect of his return to the club. 'He complained bitterly about people with no knowledge, but who because of their position were entitled to have a say in the running of the club,' his son Ian recalled. '"It drives me mad," he said.'

Things were no better on the playing field. Although Roy received an emotional standing ovation from the spectators before the club's first home match of the season, Hull lost their opening five matches. 'The whole of the Boulevard stood up together to applaud him when he walked out,' remembered the then 12-year-old Hull fan, Trevor Gibbons. After being raised on the almost mythical tales of Hull's glory years of the 1950s, Gibbons was surprised at how slight a figure Roy was: 'I'd expected a giant to come out onto the pitch,' he said.

He wasn't the only one who expected Roy to be superhuman, and this was perhaps the problem. The high expectations placed on him were in inverse proportion to the difficulties facing the team. When he returned from his leave of absence in September, Roy immediately recruited Graham Williams and Merv Hicks, two of the three British players he had signed for North Sydney. They immediately had an impact and the side won three games in a row. Over the next few weeks Roy arranged for seven Australian players to fly over to play for Hull. Only one of them, prop-forward Len Dittmar, played more than a couple of first-team games, and within a matter of weeks most had drifted home, having done nothing to improve the side.

By October it was clear to everyone that Roy's return was not working. 'We didn't have the money, we didn't have the players, and it was a long way for him to travel,' was how Peter Charlesworth summed up his dilemma. 'It was quite obvious his heart wasn't in it.' Johnny Whiteley found him 'very, very subdued' compared to how he had been before he went to Australia, and thought that his bruising experience in Australia had stripped away some of his self-confidence. 'Whereas before he was bouncing, ebullient, full of ideas,' observed Charlesworth, 'he came back more like a chastened man.' Two years in Sydney had exacted a heavy toll.

The only bright spot came in late October when Hull went to play Leeds. When Roy came out onto the pitch the Headingley crowd rose as one to salute him. As befitted his style, the two sides played a blistering match before Leeds pulled ahead to win 23-17. It was his valedictory moment. Three days later, he announced he was stepping down as coach for 'business and personal reasons'. He hinted that he might consider returning in the new year but in reality, he was just softening the blow. Everyone knew it was over.

THE COLLEGE OF CLASSICAL RUGBY
LEAGUE EDUCATION

But rugby league wasn't over for Roy. The sport was in his blood, and even the frustrations of the previous few years were not enough to extinguish his desire to be involved. As his daughter-in-law Anne remembered, 'He didn't talk very much about anything other than rugby. You didn't have a conversation with him much about anything else.' Eighteen months after his aborted return to Hull, Roy once again returned to a seat of his former glories. This time it was Leeds, where coach Eric Ashton had abruptly ended his three-year contract at the club after just one season.

Roy had kept in touch with Leeds chairman Jack Myerscough after he went to Australia in 1968, and the two became good friends when Roy and Rene returned home and moved in near to him in north Leeds. When Myerscough asked him if he would be interested in coaching again, Roy snapped his hand off. On 28 May, 1974, four days after Ashton's resignation, Leeds announced that Roy Francis was back.

He must have felt like a father returning home to his now grown-up family after a long absence. In the six years he had been away, the team of players he had created had become one of rugby league's dominant and most attractive sides. They had been champions twice, runners-up twice, and won every other trophy available to them, with the sole exception of the Challenge Cup. Some of the players he nurtured in the 1960s had retired or been transferred – most notably his 'little general' Barry Seabourne, who the club felt was injury-prone and sold to Bradford – but everyone recognised that his stamp was still deep in the DNA of the team.

The shiver of anticipation felt by Leeds' supporters was captured by the *Yorkshire Evening Post*, which announced his return with 'Roy Francis is back in his old job as principal of the Headingley College of Classical Rugby League Education'. Roy told fans he had accepted the job because:

'It offered me the opportunity to renew old and valued friendships both on and off the field at Headingley, it also presented me with the added opportunity to try and re-create possibly the most interesting, absorbing and rewarding section of my football life ... I do not for one moment think that the task is going to be an easy one (it wasn't easy in 1963) but by a dint of hard work we developed and applied spirit, dedication and the determination to rugby, which fortunately produced the sort of rugby that brought not only entertainment and success, but also respect.'

Respect, the desire for it and the need to create it, for himself and those around him, was once again at the heart of what he wanted to achieve.

He began his Headingley homecoming in his typical manner. Pre-season preparation started in early summer with three training nights a week. 'Peak physical fitness also brings the right mental attitude,' he told the journalist Trevor Watson. 'You establish discipline, and, perhaps most important, establish a knowledge of each other – coach and player.' He also looked to strengthen the team by signing Great Britain forward Mick Harrison from Hull. Slightly offended by their former coach trying to entice their best player, the Hull board resisted until Leeds, always the richest club in rugby league, overcame their resistance by offering them a record transfer fee of £10,000. Hull felt they had little choice because of their financial problems and the fact that Harrison, no doubt influenced by Roy's considerable powers of persuasion, had told them he wanted to play for Leeds.

The season started as it would continue, with Leeds unbeaten at home in the first 10 matches but struggling for convincing away performances. They finished the season third in the league, having sparkled occasionally but not consistently. 'When I joined Leeds in 1963 it took me two years to build a really good team. I've been back only a season and people have expected me to do the same in half the time,' Roy explained. He strengthened the team with experienced forwards like Harrison and the scheming scrum-half Mel Mason, but also stabilised it by persuading captain Syd Hynes, one of the original 'Roy's Boys', to delay his retirement. 'Now I know I can turn it on again, there's no need to pack in,' said Hynes, echoing the points Roy made to him. 'I'm going to stay around until the youngsters start coming through.'

The season culminated with the Premiership Trophy, a knock-out tournament for the top 16 clubs in the league. Leeds brushed aside their first three opponents and strode into the final to face St Helens. Saints had finished top of the league by a clear 11 points and had only lost three league games all season. Their coach was Eric Ashton, who had coached Leeds just 12 months earlier. They were heavy favourites.

Nevertheless, Leeds raced into an unassailable 16-0 lead at half-time by playing 'clinical but scintillating' rugby. At the end of the 80 minutes they had won the Premiership Trophy by 26-11, with the bulk of the points coming from graduates of Roy's 1960s team. This was what Leeds' fans had dreamed of, what the players wanted, and what Roy had craved since leaving the club in 1968. 'If Saturday's display is a fair indication of what is in store,' wrote an admiring John Huxley in his match report, 'then it will not be long before the Headingley club is top dog again.'

But just five days' later, the euphoria of Leeds's fans had collapsed into despair. 'Francis to leave Headingley' was the shocking *Evening Post* headline that greeted people as they left work. But their disappointment was nothing compared to the sense of betrayal felt by Roy towards those he thought were his friends.

When he joined Leeds in May 1974 he signed a one-year contract. As the end of the season approached, he became concerned that the club had not spoken to him about renewing the contract. Shortly before the last league match of the season, he wrote to the directors, asking them to clarify where he stood. 'My contract ends on May 31 and knowing the board's preference for forward planning, I would assume my services are not required for the coming season,' he wrote. 'I can assure you that every effort will be made towards winning the Premiership.'

Although he told journalist Arthur Haddock this was not a resignation letter, it's easy to imagine how the directors could have taken it, especially if they were looking to replace him. Leeds chairman Jack Myerscough claimed he had met Roy to tell him that his services were no longer required. He then claimed he had been unable to contact Roy about issuing a statement to the press – despite it being a short car journey between their homes – so he had simply left it to his secretary to do. If the pain of being abandoned by the club was not bad enough, Roy also had to deal with the betrayal of his trust by someone he considered to be a close friend.

'I can remember him being really upset,' recalled Geoff Francis. 'Jack Myerscough lived two or three hundred yards from where they were living, and got on with my father like a house on fire.' Roy understood that sentiment played no role in professional sport, but what he could not bear was the lack of respect that had been shown to him. To rub salt in the wound, Leeds immediately appointed Syd Hynes, the man Roy had persuaded not to retire from playing a few days previously, as their new player-coach. Peter Roe thought the dismissal broke Roy's heart. Leeds was a big club in a big city which not only provided the big stage on which Roy wanted to operate, but it also had the resources to enable him to be successful. When he left Leeds for the final time, it must have seemed that the door had been slammed firmly shut on his ambitions.

In hindsight, it's difficult not to conclude that Leeds had only ever intended Roy to be a temporary coach and that Hynes, a tough, inspirational captain on the field, was being groomed for the coaching role. There may also have been other contributory factors. Roy had never got on with club secretary Alf Rutherford, who he suspected of harbouring racist attitudes towards him, and the board's strict control of the team did not sit easily with Roy's belief that the coach should have complete power in all team matters. As he had seen during his previous reign at the club, no one at Leeds was bigger than the board of directors, but a successful Roy Francis would have the charisma and the authority to challenge that control. He was too big to succeed.

Once again, Roy had returned to the scene of former glories only to find disappointment. At Hull, the parlous state of the club had quickly caused him to abandon the dream of recreating the triumphs of the 1950s. Now at Leeds he had discovered that even winning was not enough. The psychological impact of his dismissal from Leeds must have been hard to bear. Being a winning coach in professional sport appeared to bring power, and power meant Roy could control his environment, shutting out racism and everything else that diminished the respect he expected for himself and gave to others. But the Leeds experience showed him that even winning was not a guarantee of control – he was always subject to the whim and caprices of club directors.

The times were changing too. As Roy's ability to create his own environment diminished, Britain in the 1970s saw racism become more overt and violent. Skinheads attacked black and Asian people, fascist marches through towns and cities became regular occurrences, and racism became a flashpoint for politics. Barely three miles from Headingley, fascist newspaper sellers openly sold their wares outside Leeds United's Elland Road ground and racist chants could be heard inside the stadium. The certainties of the past upon which Roy Francis had built his life and career were beginning to crumble.

GONE NORTHERN

Despite these disappointments, Roy still itched to be involved in the game. He didn't have to wait long for another opportunity to come along.

At the end of September 1975, little more than four months after the depressing end to his Leeds career, Bradford Northern chairman Harry Womersley rang him to ask if he was interested in taking over as coach of the club. The incumbent, Ian Brooke, had just resigned and they needed someone to rebuild the club. Roy didn't hesitate and on 2 October it was announced to the press that Roy Francis was the club's new coach.

He began in typical style by immediately ordering 36 pairs of running spikes for his new players, and making use of the speedway track that ran around the pitch at Bradford's massive Odsal stadium for sprint training. He talked about the long-term development of the club and, as he did when he first started at Leeds, slowly brought in experienced players to shore up the team while he rebuilt it. When he signed the hugely experienced prop-forward Terry Clawson it was the seventh club that Clawson had played for. When it came to Roy's trademark sprint-training, the old prop told him not to bother with his stopwatch: 'In my case you'll need a calendar,' he quipped.

For the younger players, training was not so relaxed. Peter Roe, a talented three-quarter who Roy signed in December 1975, remembered his first training session at Odsal: 'I thought I was fit, but I was a cocky young lad from Keighley, and I found out immediately that I wasn't fit at all.' He was warned by other players not to eat an evening meal before his first training session with Roy, but he ignored them and then found the session so hard that he vomited the entire contents of his stomach back up.

The new job reconnected Roy with one of his favourite players. Barry Seabourne had left Leeds in late 1971 after the club decided he was injury prone and transferred him to Bradford. By the time Roy came on board, Barry was club captain and very consciously trying to put into practice the lessons he learned under Roy at Leeds. It was not just Barry. From their time at Leeds, his wife Janice was also very aware of her responsibilities as the wife of the club captain, and this was encouraged by Rene who, for the first time since returning from Australia, began to play her old role at the club, taking charge of the players' wives and girlfriends just as she did in the couple's glory years. 'She made sure the directors put their hands in their pockets and all the wives and girlfriends went out for a meal,' recalled Janice. When Janice and Barry got married in 1970, Rene sent a congratulatory telegram to 'the captain and his skipper'. This was more than a joke. Janice remembers Rene organising a night out for Bradford wives and girlfriends. 'During the meal she tapped me on the shoulder and said, "I think you should say a few words." I said why? And she said, "Because you're the captain's wife."'

Roy hoped he could recreate the family environment he had at Hull in the 1950s and Leeds in the 1960s, but Bradford was a troubled club. Roy was its tenth coach in just 11 years. Despite having some success, his predecessor Ian Brooke had been forced out by the hostility of the club's supporters. There was also widespread demoralisation among the players, and the boardroom was a seething mess of intrigue and labyrinthine politics. Roy soon became frustrated with the club's part-time set-up. He only saw the players on Tuesday and Thursday evenings for training, and he struggled to establish some continuity and culture. He also fell out with club director Norman Jowett, who objected to Roy inviting Geoff Francis to travel with him on the team bus to matches.

As Peter Roe would later point out, there was also a problem about which Roy could do absolutely nothing. Bradford's Odsal stadium sat at the bottom of a deep bowl, which shielded the pitch from the sun and made drainage difficult. All the club's matches and training sessions were held on it, which meant the turf was regularly churned up. It could not provide the hard, fast surface needed for open rugby. Bradford's most successful teams were always based on big heavy forwards who battered their way up the middle of the pitch, rather than moving the ball out to the flanks. Roy's signature free-flowing 'total rugby league' style of play was almost impossible once the season reached November and the pitch turned into a thick brown porridge of mud.

By the time Christmas arrived, Bradford were still rooted in the relegation zone of the First Division (rugby league had introduced a two-division league system in 1973). Nevertheless, Roy's emphasis on fitness and his combination of youthful talent and veteran experience eventually began to pay off. An Easter resurrection saw them win seven out of their last eight matches and clamber up to mid-table respectability. The directors rewarded Roy, who had been employed on a week-week basis, with a one-year contract for the 1976–77 season.

However, in September 1976, before the new season was a fortnight old, the press reported that Roy had been admitted to hospital for a cartilage operation and had temporarily passed the coaching duties to Barry Seabourne and reserve team coach Dave Stockwell. He would be back in three weeks. But he didn't return until 31 October.

In fact, Roy was recovering after a long period of heavy drinking. He had become close to Peter Roe – like Johnny Whiteley and

Barry Seabourne, a talented and intelligent young player who Roy identified as a future leader – and as well as mentoring him, Roy also confided in him. Roe remembers Roy drinking heavily after matches, always downing pints with a spirit chaser. Roy had always enjoyed a drink – his son Geoff remembered when he was 15 and had to drive his father back home after he'd had one too many with players after training – but now he could become angry and abusive. At other times, alcohol allowed him to tell Roe about the racist abuse he had suffered and how it had affected his life. It seems that the setbacks he had experienced since his time at North Sydney had severely dented his self-confidence, and reduced his ability to shut out the racism around him.

This reached its nadir during a match against Hull at Odsal. Until the 1980s, Odsal's dressing rooms were at the top of the stadium's bowl. To get up and down to the pitch players and coaches had to walk through the crowd. This meant they were viewed as fair game for supporters to vent their grievances or prejudices as they made their way up through the spectators. Roy was sitting with Peter Roe on the players' bench and, as the end of the match loomed, he leaned over and said to Peter Roe, 'I just can't handle walking up the hill.' Shocked, not least because here was the Master Coach confessing his problems to a 21-year-old player, Roe nevertheless reassured him. 'Don't worry, Roy, I'll protect you,' he said and the two of them eventually made it through the crowd without incident. Roe knew exactly what was paralysing Roy: 'He'd been abused because of racism and because of that abuse he didn't want to do it.'

When Roy returned from drying out, the club carried on as if nothing had happened. Perhaps unsurprisingly in the circumstances, it turned out to be a disappointing season for the team. It bobbed around in the middle of the First Division and made no impact on the cup competitions. It would have ended anti-climatically if it were not for Roy being taken ill. This may again have been due to drinking but whatever the cause, his doctor told him to rest for a month. That took him to the end of his one-year contract and so he announced that he would step down as coach. The Bradford directors accepted his decision and thanked him for his services.

The club moved on, but for Peter Roe, Roy had played a pivotal role in his life. He was a 'fatherly figure,' Roe remembered almost 50 years later. 'My dad died when I was young. Roy gave me advice I wouldn't get elsewhere, fatherly advice that had an impact.' Just as with Johnny Whiteley and many other Hull and Leeds players, the influence he had on the young Roe would stay with him long after his rugby career was over.

There was almost one last hurrah. In March 1978 Roy accepted a coaching consultancy position with Second Division team Huddersfield, and told the press that if he passed a medical on the cartilage injury in his right knee he would become the club's new full-time coach. A fortnight later, he relayed the news that his injury showed no signs of improving and that meant he would not be able to take up the coaching position. Even so, this very light sprinkling of Francis magic was enough to see the club promoted to the First Division. Although he didn't know it, the curtain had come down on his unparalleled rugby league career.

RETURN TO HEADINGLEY

Life without the game proved to be increasingly difficult for Roy. He and Rene left the Buckles in the mid-1970s, as it fell victim to long-term roadworks which blocked access, changing drinking habits, and the sheer amount of work required to keep it going. In 1983 they sold their house in Leeds and moved into a rented flat. Every day, Roy would dress smartly in a shirt, tie and blazer but spend most of the time smoking and watching television. He left the running of his cafe businesses to his sons and their wives, occasionally played golf, and sometimes went to the local gym, but he and Rene rarely went out or socialised with other people. He clashed with family members, and took umbrage at the suggestion that he might like to volunteer his services to local schools or amateur rugby league teams. Even some of his old friends became reluctant to contact him. Peter Roe eventually gave up calling him; he never knew whether Roy would be friendly or antagonistic, and found him increasingly bitter at being forgotten by the world.

He did make an attempt to get on the sportsmen's after-dinner speaking circuit, and his old friend Roland Davis arranged a number of appearances for him. But, despite being a wonderful raconteur in private, Roy couldn't – or wouldn't – follow the traditional after-dinner formula of behind-the-scenes revelations and off-colour jokes, and instead discussed tactics and team preparation. He was rarely invited back. Nor, despite being one of the most articulate people in British sport, could he break into the media. Although he couldn't have known it at the time, when he fell out with Eddie Waring in the 1940s he scuppered his chances of working for the BBC as long as Eddie was its league commentator, and he was now too mistrusting of journalists to have a newspaper column ghostwritten for him.

His only attempt to engage with the BBC was when, somewhat bizarrely, he met with Peter Charlesworth to discuss suing the corporation because he believed it had stolen the format for *A Question of Sport* from an idea he had while in Sydney. Not only would this be impossible to prove in court, it was also the case that the BBC had aired a pilot of the show in 1968 before Roy even set foot in Australia.

Like many men who retired before they thought it was their time, Roy longed for the return of the recognition he had enjoyed in the past. When the telephone rang in the Francis flat, an increasingly rare occurrence as the decade dragged on for the couple, he would joke to Rene as she went to answer it: 'If that's the *Daily Mail*, tell them I'm not in!' He meant the *Hull Daily Mail*, not the national newspaper, an echo from the time when in the 1950s he would appear regularly on its front page, a bittersweet memory of the era when he was the King of West Hull.

But if Roy had faded from popular memory, 'The Francis Formula' style of total rugby league had come very much into the public eye. In 1982 the Australian Kangaroos touring team visited Britain and astounded fans with their dynamic style of play. This was truly a team built on Roy's principles. Big forwards could run and pass like backs, with backs who could tackle as hard as forwards. A player like second-row forward Wayne Pearce was a

new age Johnny Whiteley, and scrum-half Peter Sterling was the
very definition of Roy's ideal of a scheming general, just as Barry
Seabourne had been for him in the 1960s. Indeed, Roy may have
had some influence on the rapid tactical evolution which took
place in Australian rugby league in the 1970s. When he was at
North Sydney, Jack Gibson, universally acknowledged as Australia's
master coach, would ring him every week to discuss the weekend's
matches. 'He's picking my brains,' Roy told Jim Mills. Whatever
pickings Gibson got, they served him well as he went on to win
five premiership titles in Australia, including a hat-trick with a
Parramatta side which played such innovative attacking rugby they
could have been mistaken for a Roy Francis team.

In 1985 the redoubtable Ian Heads, editor of Sydney's *Rugby
League Week*, dispatched Neil Cadigan to England to cover the
influx of Australian stars who were playing in the British game in
the aftermath of that historic Kangaroo tour. As well as covering
the household name players, Heads told Cadigan to try to track
down Roy Francis, 'The man they drove from town' as the interview
would be headlined. Cadigan found his man to be charismatic,
witty and remarkably fit-looking for someone in his mid-sixties.
For one of the few times in his life, Roy spoke publicly about the
racism he faced in Australia, gratified by the interest and sympathy
shown to him by Cadigan. The following year, Roy was one of
seven great Welsh players featured in Robert Gate's groundbreaking
book *Gone North*, which chronicled the exploits of those players
who made their way from the Welsh valleys to find glory in the
North of England. Roy was someone, argued Gate, who showed
that 'entertainment and winning are not incompatible' and that
'style and success, even in a game dominated by violent physical
confrontation, can be synonymous', words that could have come
straight from the man himself. In 1988, the journalist Ian Proctor
conducted a wide-ranging interview with him for the sport's trade
paper, the *Rugby Leaguer*. In the autumn of his life, Roy's reputation
had begun to flower again.

However, in the spring of 1989, two months after his 70th
birthday, Roy collapsed with chest pains while playing golf. Doctors

diagnosed he was suffering from an abdominal aortic aneurysm –
a bulge in the artery which carries blood from the heart – and
surgery was arranged to take place at St James's Hospital in Leeds
on Friday 31 March.

A few days before he was due to be admitted into hospital, a
new Leeds rugby league 'Wall of Fame' was unveiled at Headingley.
Roy had been invited but both Rene and his doctor advised him
against attending and suggested he should rest before he went into
hospital. But Roy was determined to be there. This was to be a
celebration of all that was great about Leeds rugby league, and he
knew that not only would his time at the club be honoured, but
also that the players he had mentored and raised would likewise be
lauded. He could not miss it.

It turned out to be a wonderful occasion. He was greeted as the
returning hero and praised to the skies. Drink flowed, memories
were shared, and the years melted away as ageing men recalled the
deeds of their younger selves. The bonds they had forged decades
ago re-emerged as strong as ever, rekindled by the exaggerations of
memory and the experiences of lives lived after rugby. Roy even got
up to sing, just like he used to after matches in the 1960s when he
would lock the pub doors and the players and their wives continued
to celebrate into the small hours of the morning. He was back home,
and it felt like he had never left. Did it perhaps then cross his mind
that he should never have left Leeds for North Sydney?

No doubt he expected to have plenty of time to reminisce when
he checked into St James's Hospital later that week. Surgery to
repair a heart aneurysm is serious but usually successful, and Roy
expected to be out of hospital and at home recuperating in a few
days. Within a couple of hours of arriving, he was prepped for
surgery and the anaesthetic administered.

His aorta was successfully repaired and the operation seemed
to have been a success. But as he lay in his hospital bed waiting to
recover, his blood pressure shot up, he began to bleed internally,
and he lost consciousness. Over the next five days, his kidneys and
then his heart failed. On Wednesday 5 April, 1989, Roy Lionel
Francis died.

The Leader's Legacy

'I loved Roy.'

The funeral was a happy, joyous celebration of Roy's life and the impact he had made on the lives of those who knew him.

Appropriately it took place just a couple of miles from Headingley stadium at Lawnswood cemetery in north Leeds. There was competition between his former players over who should be a pall-bearer, and it seemed each of the more than one hundred people who were there had their own inspirational story to tell about their departed leader. If a person's value could be measured by the lasting memories of those they left behind, Roy's treasure would be limitless.

Rene saw out the millennium and died on 6 January, 2000, aged 85. Although illness and infirmity gradually took over, there were still occasions when she would bump into a former player and reminisce over a drink about the times when she and Roy commanded all they surveyed. Like the illegitimate mixed-race boy she married, she had come a long way from the girl who sold sweets door-to-door in the hungry thirties. Neither of them could have imagined how their lives would unfold or that they would leave such a legacy.

Some of that legacy could be seen in the players Roy had coached, who themselves became coaches. From Hull, Johnny Whiteley and Colin Hutton both went on to coach Great Britain,

Tommy Harris led York for many years, and Ivor Watts coached Hull before being replaced by Roy in 1972. From Leeds, Robin Dewhurst and Sid Hynes followed in his footsteps and coached Leeds, Barry Seabourne spent 14 years at the head of three clubs, while Phil Holmes went on to a distinguished coaching career at all levels of the game. Peter Roe coached eight clubs over almost 30 years, and never once forgot what he had learned under Roy. The Francis Formula did not die with its creator.

Just as importantly, Roy's name was indelibly associated with the fast, open rugby he coached and loved. A couple of years after he left Bradford, the team unexpectedly ran in several tries before half-time in a league match. Peter Fox, who had replaced Roy as coach and whose name was synonymous with old-school forward-based rugby, greeted the players as they came into the dressing room with the words, 'Bloody hell, everyone will be saying we're playing Roy Francis rugby!'

'Roy Francis rugby' brought success to Roy's teams, to his players, and for his philosophy of how rugby should be played. Most importantly, it also brought him the thing he valued the most: respect. Alongside his innovations and leadership skills, his triumph as a coach was based on treating his players well. The harsh disciplinary attitude of most sports coaches was alien to Roy's way of dealing with his players. He treated people as he himself expected to be treated, with respect and dignity. To treat people in the best possible way was to fill them with the confidence to be their best possible selves, on and off the field.

However, the sad truth was that respect and dignity could not be guaranteed to a black man like Roy in a racist society. The unique, albeit limited, space that rugby league provided for black players – exemplified at the time of Roy's death by the magisterial Ellery Hanley's captaincy of Great Britain – gave Roy the opportunity to develop his athletic talents and then, as a coach, to create an environment which he could control and build a team based on the mutual respect he valued above all else.

But once that control was breached, the tides of racism started to seep in around him. At North Sydney, Roy found himself at the mercy of the Sydney press, who never allowed him to forget the colour of his skin. When he returned to England in 1971, the influence he had in the 1950s and 1960s had been weakened by changing times and the vicissitudes of club officials. Deprived of the huge authority that his methods and success had brought him in the earlier decades, he became an ordinary black man, subject to the whim of those who judged him by nothing but his colour.

Like his father Lionel, Roy could never reconcile himself to a racist world. In contrast to Lionel, who raged against his surroundings until he found politics in the United States, Roy sought to escape the world of racial discrimination by exerting complete control over his environment. He tried to make himself independent of the outside world through his teams and his businesses. He wanted to be beholden to no one, whether in sport or business, and live a life beyond the reach of racial discrimination and humiliation.

So it was no accident that Rene and his sons felt that Roy was always on the move. He moved from business to business and from home to home, perpetually looking for ways to raise himself, endlessly looking for something better, forever seeking to outrun the racism which pursued him. Despite his best efforts and his great talent, he could not seal himself off from the outside world, and he could never banish the ever-present fear of discrimination. Like the protagonist in Robert Johnson's classic blues song, he knew there was a hellhound on his trail and he was determined that it would never catch up with him. But it sometimes did, at a cost of great mental torment.

When confronted with such a unique and extraordinary talent, it is tempting to suggest that Roy was a one-off, a man so gifted and so charismatic that his career was unrepresentative and can tell us nothing about race in sport or British society. But this is to downplay his struggle to make it to the top of his sport and the obstacles he had to overcome. Moreover, he was not the only black player of his generation to make it to the highest levels of rugby league. His fellow Welshman Alec Givvons predated him as a coach when he took charge of Oldham's reserve team in 1948. Roy was followed as a first-team coach by Cec Thompson, who coached

Barrow in 1959, and numerous other black British coaches such as Frank Wilson, Colin Dixon, Clive Sullivan, Bak Diabira, David Plange, Leon Pryce, Jermaine Coleman, Joe Mbu, and Ellery Hanley, who in 1994 became the first black head coach of any British national team. Roy needed his talent and determination to succeed, but without rugby league he would not have the arena in which he could make the most of his talents.

But being a pioneer in sport does not mean that others will necessarily follow, nor that progress is irreversible. At the time of writing, there were no black British head coaches at any professional British rugby league club. The memory of past achievements may be obscuring the problems of the present. Even worse, in rugby union, only one black British coach, Paul Hull, has ever held the reins at a leading British club. In soccer, black managers were almost unknown until the 21st century, with the exception of Rochdale's Tony Collins in the 1960s and Lincoln's Keith Alexander in the 1990s. Even today, only four black Britons have ever held permanent managerial positions in the Premier League. The celebration of 'firsts' – such as the first black professional or the first black international player – too often ignores the fact that 'first' implies a continuing sequence, and that solitary instances of black players or coaches are often merely isolated exceptions. Without a society based on the principles of human equality – where black, white and all people of colour can mix as they did in a Roy Francis-coached team – change will only ever be temporary and provisional.

All lives end in death, and most lives fade in their closing years. The chronology of life means that biographies almost inevitably end on a note of sadness. Yet despite his decline in his last decade, the story of Roy Francis should not be left at that. His was an extraordinary life of achievement, unparalleled for his generation of working-class black Britons. One of the finest rugby players of the 1940s, a creator of two of rugby league's greatest club sides, and the founder of modern rugby coaching, his name deserves to be elevated to one of the most important pioneers of sport and black British history. He should no longer be the forgotten black leader.

Almost 30 years after his death, and over 80 years since he left Brynmawr for Wigan, Roy's achievements began to be recognised in Wales. In 2018 he was inducted into the Welsh Sports' Hall of Fame and then, in late October 2023, his memory was honoured in his hometown. Hundreds of people from across Wales and England gathered on a wet Saturday morning in Brynmawr town centre to witness the unveiling of a statue of the man who had become its most famous son. As the ceremony began, the rain stopped and the sun began to shine as Roy's elder son Geoff and dual-code Welsh rugby legend Jonathan Davies revealed the statue to the world. As if to emphasise the link between the world in which he had grown up and the world in which he had achieved so much, the day brought together for the first time Roy's Yorkshire-born great-grandchildren with the descendants of his cousins who stayed in the Welsh valleys and continued the 140-year history of Brynmawr's black and mixed-race community.

At long last Roy Francis had been given due respect by the town in which he had grown up.

Yet even that civic honour and the growing public appreciation of his achievements could barely begin to compare with the private gratitude of those he had led and mentored over his decades as a rugby league coach. For those players, Roy was a fatherly figure who helped them to unlock the true extent of their talents, provided the team platform for their success, and helped them to live fuller lives. It was not enough to dream, he told them, the important thing was to be able to create memories. No one understood or expressed this better than Johnny Whiteley, whose affection for Roy and how he had changed his life still burned brightly more than 70 years after they had first met: 'Kids like me didn't know what we could be because we'd never been introduced to anything, and I look back on that and think how many kids had so much ability but got bypassed. That's where I was lucky. I loved Roy and I couldn't thank him enough.'

Acknowledgements

First and foremost, I am deeply indebted to Roy's sons, Geoff and Ian, and their wives, Anne and Jean, for allowing me into their family's history and for providing so much personal insight into the lives of their father and mother. This book could not have been written without them. Sadly, Geoff Francis died in January 2025 so did not live to see publication of the book to which he had contributed so much.

I would also like to thank the many other people who gave interviews, provided insights, or assisted in some way with the research: Geoff Armstrong, Steve Ball, Rebecca Bowd, Drew Broatch, Val Broatch, Neil Cadigan, Geoff Caplan, Phil Caplan, Ros Caplan, Neil Carter, Peter Charlesworth, James Clarke, Steve Coombes, Bill Dalton, Ann Dardaine, Roland Davis, Margaret Dewhurst, Robin Dewhurst, Laura Dixon, Simon Foster, Cathy France, Rhiannon Garth-Jones, Robert Gate, Trevor Gibbons, Alan Golding, Nick Halafihi, Peter Harvey, Ian Haywood, Gary Hetherington, Caroline Hitt, Phil Holmes, Syd Hynes, Lisa Jones, Spencer Kassimir, Mike Latham, Simon Lenagan, Joan Livesey, Eifion Lloyd Davies, Peter Lush, Roy Masters, Jim Mills, Andrew Moore, Graham Morris, Neil Ormston, Keith Pollard, Ian Proctor, Mark Rees, Mel Reuben, Peter Roe, Angela Saunderson, Barry Seabourne, Janice Seabourne, Stuart Sheard, Bernard Shooman, Patrick Skene, Alan Smith, Jarrod Steadman, Keith Sutch, David Thorpe, Keith Tindall, Alyson Tippings, Martin Whitcombe, Johnny Whiteley, Simon Wilkinson and Andy Wilson. A number of friends and experts read the manuscript and provided their particular specialist expertise which helped improve the book immensely, especially Dr Victoria Dawson, Sean McGuire, Martin Offiah, Huw Richards and Terry Williams. Needless to say, any mistakes, errors or omissions are the fault of the author alone. Finally, I'd like to acknowledge the influence of my parents and grandparents, citizens of the same world as Roy, who also helped to create the Hull in which he lived, and for whom Roy Francis was an exemplar of local pride and the sport of rugby league.

References

Unless otherwise stated, all interviews were conducted in person between July 2021 and February 2024.

INTRODUCTION

'Somewhere between what a man does': Roy Francis, *Rugby League World* (Sydney), April 1969.

CHAPTER ONE

'I am not willing to suffer': Lionel Francis, *South Wales Gazette*, 25 January, 1906.

'One of 50 black miners': *Dundee Evening Post*, 24 July, 1900.

'We were all the same colour anyway': Charlie Williams, *Ee – I've Had Some Laughs* (Wolfe Publishing Ltd., London, 1973) 22.

'They were judged not on their colour': Alfred Lawes interview 1998, https://www.bl.uk/collection-items/rhondda-valley-accent-alfred -father, accessed 12 February, 2020. For black miners in Wales, see also Rebecca and Paul Eversley, *Calypso and Coal* (Historic Dock Project, Cardiff, 2023).

'Found guilty and fined five shillings': *South Wales Gazette*, 21 December, 1906.

'He reluctantly accepted the fine': *South Wales Gazette*, 25 January, 1906.

'Should Black Man Marry White Woman?': *South Wales Gazette*, 24 August, 1900.

'Objections to the plaintiff's race': *Cardiff Times*, 22 April, 1905.

'Married life had not been very pleasant': *South Wales Gazette*, 18 October, 1918.

'Jerry Shea and his teammate': *Western Mail*, 21 June, 3 and 4 July, 1919.

'Givvons' father was later detained': Laura Tabili, *'We Ask for British Justice': Workers and Racial Difference in Late Imperial Britain* (Cornell University Press, London, 1994) 216.

'Bluntly refused on account of our colour': quoted in Jacqueline Jenkinson, *Black 1919: Riots, Racism and Resistance in Imperial Britain* (Oxford Academic, Liverpool, 2009) 192.

'Uncompromising attitude towards white people': Kenneth Little, *Negroes in Britain: A Study of Racial Relations in English Society* (Routledge & Kegan Paul, London, 1972) 57.

'Vivid recollection of race riots': *Picture Post*, 22 April, 1950.

'Persistent cruelty had not been proved': *South Wales Gazette*, 20 April, 1920.

'Over 400,000 people abandoned hope': Kenneth O. Morgan, *Rebirth of a Nation: A History of Modern Wales, 1880–1980* (Oxford University Press, Oxford, 1987) 211–13.

'Spiritual distress been so acute': Hilda Jennings, *Brynmawr: A Study of a Distressed Area* (Allenson & Co. Ltd., London, 1934) 10.

'Half of the town's working population': Morgan, *Rebirth of a Nation: A History of Modern Wales, 1880–1980* (Oxford University Press, Oxford, 1987) 225.

'Another 20 per cent had to leave Brynmawr': Hilda Jennings, *Brynmawr: A Study of a Distressed Area* (Allenson & Co. Ltd., London, 1934) 144–49; see also the undated pamphlet *A Town on the Dole* published by the Brynmawr branch of the Communist Party.

'Pelted the police with stones': *The Times*, 22 March, 1935.

'Reduced to a bare subsistence level': Kenneth Little, *Negroes in Britain: A Study of Racial Relations in English Society* (Routledge & Kegan Paul, London, 1972) 78 and 257.

'Ordered to pay the costs of the case': *Merthyr Express*, 29 June, 1929.

'A stronger antidote to this poison': James Baldwin, *Notes of a Native Son* (Beacon Press, London, 1958) 107.

'The unhappy fate of he who is neither black nor white': Chamion Caballero and Peter J. Aspinall, *Mixed Race Britain in the Twentieth Century* (Palgrave Macmillan, London, 2018) 33.

'Moral standards are extraordinarily low': Mark Christian, 'The Fletcher Report 1930: A Historical Case Study of Contested Black Mixed Heritage Britishness', *Journal of Historical Sociology* (2008) 1:2/3; Peter J. Aspinall, 'The Social Evolution of the Term "Half-Caste" in Britain: The Paradox of its Use as Both Derogatory Racial Category and Self-Descriptor', *Journal of Historical Sociology* (2013) 26:4; see also *Negro World*, 23 August, 1930.

'Anxious to preserve his self-respect': D. F. Kanaka, 'The Colour Bar in Britain', *The Spectator*, 30 March, 1934.

'Fifty years after the publication': Mark Christian, 'The Fletcher Report 1930', 222.

'Since the start of the 20th century Harlem had become': Winston James, *Claude McKay: The Making of a Black Bolshevik* (Columbia University Press, New York, 2022) 201; The *New York Age* of 11 February, 1933, estimated that 17 per cent of Harlem's population were born outside of the USA, mainly from the West Indies.

'The dark warm throbbing bosom of Harlem': James, *Claude McKay: The Making of a Black Bolshevik* (Columbia University Press, New York, 2022) 210.

'Banned in several British colonies': Monthly Review of Revolutionary Movements in British Dominions Overseas and Foreign Countries, August 1920, no. 22, 26, in TNA CAB-24-112a.

'How Lionel became a delegate': He is listed as Lionel Antonio Francis in Hill et al., The Marcus Garvey and UNIA Papers, vol. 2, p. 682.

'President of the city's UNIA branch': *Negro World*, 5 August, 1922.

'Dr Lionel Francis, a physician': *Pittsburgh Courier*, 18 October and 15 August, 1925. He does not appear in the alumni lists of any of his claimed alma maters.

'East African School of Medicine and Surgery': *Philadelphia Inquirer*, 30 April, 1922.

'In April 1922 he was taken to court': *Philadelphia Inquirer*, 30 April, 1922.

'The chiropractors called the police': *Philadelphia Inquirer*, 11 and 12 June, 1922.

'Three months in jail and fined $100': *Kingston Whig-Standard*, 29 September, 1922.

'Worked closely with Marcus Garvey': *Pittsburgh Courier*, 14 June, 1924.

'Dr Lionel Francis Tells Why He Quit': *New York Age*, 30 August, 1924.

'Branches in Philadelphia and New York': *Pittsburgh Courier*, 18 October, 1924.

'Offered medical and dental facilities': *Pittsburgh Courier*, 15 August, 1925.

'A political organisation of a different character': *Pittsburgh Courier*, 20 February, 1926.

'Honest, very active and willing': letters from Charles H. Knapp, 11 January, 1934 and Graham Churchward, 5 November, 1934, in possession of Geoff and Anne Francis.

'Captain of the Invincibles': *Merthyr Express*, 21 February, 1931; letter from G. N. Morgan, 1 November, 1934.

'Trainer to Gipsy Daniels': *Hull Daily Mail*, 10 August, 1957.

'The new outdoor swimming pool': Over 160 lidos were opened in Britain in the 1930s, see Daryl Leeworthy, *Workers' Fields: sport, landscape, and the Labour movement in South Wales, 1858–1958*, PhD thesis, University of Swansea, 2011.

'Roy finished third in a 120 yards sprint': *Merthyr Express*, 26 August, 1933.

'The premier sporting institution': Hilda Jennings, *Brynmawr: A Study of a Distressed Area* (Allenson & Co. Ltd., London, 1934) 133.

'Roy Francis, the left wing, showed much promise': *Merthyr Express*, 19 September, 1936.

'He had "a great future"': *Merthyr Express*, 26 September, 1936.

'Once again Roy earned praise': *Merthyr Express*, 3 and 10 October, 1936.

'The scout was Arthur Fairfax': Alun Richards, *Carwyn: A Personal Memoir* (Michael Joseph, London, 1984) 87–88; Simon Foster, Robert Gate and Peter Lush, *Trevor Foster: The Life of a Rugby League Legend* (London League Publications Ltd., London, 2005) 11.

'"Lionel Roy Francis, centre three-quarter," had signed for the club': *Wigan Observer*, 17 November, 1936.

CHAPTER TWO

'A second- or third-rate side': *Wigan Examiner*, 16 October 1926.

'A miserable picture of the town and its people': George Orwell, *The Road to Wigan Pier* (Penguin Modern Classics, Harmondsworth, 1972) 75 and 43.

'Wiganers are passionately keen on education': Douglas Macdonald Hastings, 'Wigan', *Picture Post*, 11 November 1939, 13–21.

'Its famous pies': Jeffrey P. Green, 'Beef pie with a suet crust: a black childhood in Wigan (1906–20)', *New Community* vol. 11, no. 3 (1984) 291–8.

'Only three players of African descent': Bill Hern and David Gleave, *Football's Black Pioneers: The Stories of the First Black Players to Represent the 92 League Clubs* (Conker Editions Ltd., Leicester, 2020).

'Records remain frustratingly sparse': *The Leader*, 21 June, 1929; *The Keys*, July 1937, 25.

'A black man taking the place of a white man': *Manchester Evening News*, 9 July, 1975; Jeffrey Hill, *Learie Constantine and Race Relations in Britain and the Empire* (Bloomsbury 3PL, London, 2019) 56.

'The historical record has yet to be thoroughly investigated': *Hull Daily Mail*, 5 June, 1922; *Sheffield Daily Telegraph*, 9 June, 1930.

'I'd never seen so many mixed-race couples': James Oddy, *True Professional: The Clive Sullivan Story* (Pitch Publishing Ltd., Worthing, 2017) 125.

'A freezing out in athletics': *The Keys*, July 1937.

'Learie Constantine fought a famous legal case': Jeffrey Hill, *Learie Constantine and Race Relations in Britain and the Empire* (Bloomsbury Academic, London, 2019) 102–7.

'Virtually impossible to book hotel rooms': *Daily Herald*, 22 December 1937.

'It remained in place until 1948': Shirin Hirsch and Geoff Brown, 'Breaking the "colour bar": Len Johnson, Manchester and anti-racism', Race & Class (Sage Journals, 2023) 64:3.

'Francis brought off two excellent tackles': *Wigan Examiner*, 24 November, 1936.

'Calling him a star': *Wigan Observer*, 19 April, 1937; Peter Lush, *Ahead of His Time: Roy Francis and Rugby League* (London League Publications Ltd., London, 2022) 7.

'22.5 per cent of all women who got married': Pat Thane, 'Happy Families? History and Family Policy' (The British Academy, London, 2010) 48.

'When jazz singer Cleo Laine's white mother': Graham Collier, *Cleo and John: Biography of Cleo Laine and John Dankworth* (Quartet Books, London, 1974) 24.

'A thing of horror': Letter to *The Times*, 14 June, 1919.

'Menace of Mixed Unions': *Daily Herald*, 10 January 1929; *Western Mail*, 23 January 1929; *Daily Telegraph*, 16 June, 1930.

'Sunderland was an engine driver's son': For Sunderland's career in Australia, see Max and Reed Howell, *The Centenary of the Greatest Game Under the Sun: One Hundred Years of Rugby League in Queensland* (Celebrity Books, Queensland, 1989).

'Suggest you accept the Wigan offer': *Maryborough Chronicle* (Queensland) 16 December, 1937.

'His salary was an astronomical £400 a year': *Courier-Mail* (Brisbane), 9 August 1938.

'He is a stylist…': *Wigan Examiner*, 28 January, 1939.

'Racialism is like pain': Roy Francis, *Sunday Telegraph* (Sydney),
    11 April, 1971.

'Wigan Need New Centre': *Manchester Evening News*, 19 August, 1939.

'Francis did not make any progress': *Brisbane Telegraph*, 11 February, 1939.

'How sad it is that there are not more Germans like them': *Brisbane
    Telegraph*, 21 August, 1939.

CHAPTER THREE

'You not only had to make their bodies right but their minds right as
    well': Roy Francis in the *Daily Mirror*, 23 March, 1968.

'I like Francis': *North-Western Daily Mail*, 16 January, 1939.

'They were all against him': *Lancashire Daily Post*, 23 June and 5 August,
    1925.

'A candidate for the Australian tour': *Lancashire Evening Post*, 14
    October, 1935.

'Roy Francis is a star': *Barrow News & Mail*, 27 January, 1939.

'Only men of "pure European descent"': Marika Sherwood, *Many
    Struggles: West Indian Workers and Service Personnel in Britain,
    1939–45* (Karia Press, London, 1985) 1–2.

'George Price was turned down by the Royal Navy': *Daily Record*,
    11 January 1940.

'We had anticipated Herr Hitler': *The Scotsman*, 15 May, 1939.

'Colour bar would be lifted': Sherwood, *Many Struggles: West Indian
    Workers and Service Personnel in Britain, 1939–45* (Karia Press,
    London, 1985) 5–6.

'Obviously men of colour': Gavin Schaffer 'Re-Thinking the History
    of Blame: Britain and Minorities during the Second World War',
    National Identities, 8:4 (2006) 414.

'Almost 15 hours one way': John Schleppi, *Rugby League in Wartime*
    (PhD thesis, University of Dayton, 1981) 62.

'Even the great Brian Bevan': undated clipping in Ian Francis' scrapbook.

'Roy's friend Trevor Foster': Foster, Gate and Lush, *Trevor Foster: The
    Life of a Rugby League Legend* (London League Publications Ltd.,
    London, 2005) 23; Gary James, *Joe Mercer OBE: Football with a
    Smile* (James Ward, Manchester, 1993) 46.

'Promote comradeship and create "team spirit"': *Army Physical Training
    Corps Basic and Battle Physical Training* (H. M. S. O., London, 1944) 7.

'Arsenal centre-forward Tommy Lawton': E. A. L. Oldfield, *History of the Army Physical Training Corps* (Gale and Polden, Aldershot, 1955); Nikolai Bogdanovic, *Fit to Fight: A History of the Royal Army Physical Training Corps 1860–2015* (Osprey Publishing, Oxford, 2017).

'Agility, dexterity and speed': *Army Physical Training Corps Basic and Battle Physical Training* (H. M. S. O., London, 1944) 5–6; for the influence of the Army Physical Training Corps on football managers, see Neil Carter, *The Football Manager: A History* (Routledge, Abingdon-on-Thames, 2006) 85.

'You had to start with the brain': *Daily Mirror*, 23 March, 1968.

'This was the stuff of which coaches are made': *Daily Mirror*, 25 March, 1968.

'His authority was largely accepted': E. I. Ekpenyon, *Some Experiences of an African Air-Raid Warden* (Sheldon Press, London, 1943) 6–9.

'Operate radios on the front lines': See Ron Goldstein's memories at https://www.bbc.co.uk/history/ww2peopleswar/stories/53/a2065853 .shtml

'Major Sloane was the officer in charge': Foster interviewed in Trevor Gibbons, 'Roy Francis' in Tony Collins and Phil Melling (eds), *The Glory of Their Times: Crossing the Colour Line in Rugby League* (Vertical Editions, Skipton, 2003) 42.

'Deceptive running of Francis': *The Scotsman*, 1 March, 1943.

'Hey, Charlie, this is playing for England!': John Schleppi, *Rugby League in Wartime* (PhD thesis, University of Dayton, 1981) 62–3.

'Prettiest try of the match': *Western Mail*, 10 April, 1944.

'Broke a leg and tore his ligaments': *Halifax Courier*, 23 August, 1944.

'The end of his playing career': *Hull Daily Mail*, 10 August, 1957.

CHAPTER FOUR

'I was fortunate to realise my ambition': *Rugby League Gazette*, October 1949.

'One of the best three-quarters in the game': *Yorkshire Post*, 22 December, 1947.

'Australia still operated a colour bar': Robert Gate, 'Roy Francis', Code 13, June 1989, 4.

'The cleverest half-back in England': *Daily Standard* (Brisbane), 2 March, 1936.

'One of the finest outside half backs': *Yorkshire Observer*, 9 January, 1936.

'The supremely gifted Stan Brogden': *Halifax Evening Courier*, 25
    January, 1936.
'If players are selected on merit': *Daily* Standard, 2 March, 1936.
'Colour Deprived Bennett of Tour': *Daily* Standard, 5 March, 1936.
'Colour Line in Rugby League': *Auckland Star*, 5 March, 1936
'We had the West Indies [cricket] team here': *Australian Worker*, 11
    March, 1936.
'The colour bar is a difficult one': *Yorkshire Observer*, 9 January, 1936.
'As Welshman of colour, was not chosen': *Yorkshire Observer*, 8
    December, 1937.
'A group of selectors who would not select Givvons': *Bradford Observer*,
    9 December, 1937.
'So richly coloured a rite of passage': *Canberra Times*, 27 May, 1979.
'Local supporter Willie Mann': John Schleppi, *Rugby League in
    Wartime* (PhD thesis, University of Dayton, 1981) 112.
'The negotiations with Hunslet': *Yorkshire Evening Post*, 29 May, 1948;
    Halifax Evening Courier, 12 July, 1948.
'I refused to turn Herbert out': Anthony Richmond, *Colour Prejudice
    in Britain: A Study of West Indian Workers in Liverpool, 1941–51*
    (Routledge, Abingdon-on-Thames, 1954) 89.
'Nat Bookbinder was then called up': *Daily Record*, 7 December, 1943.
    Janet Toole, 'GIs and the race bar in wartime Warrington', *History
    Today* (July 1993) 43:7.
'Mixed-race babies in the area': Rose, Sonya O., 'Girls and GIs: Race,
    Sex, and Diplomacy in Second World War Britain', *The International
    History Review* (1997) 19:1.
'Brown babies': Lucy Bland, *Britain's 'Brown Babies': The Stories of
    Children Born to Black GIs and White Women in the Second World War*
    (Manchester University Press, Manchester, 2019).
'The referee failed to turn up': *Yorkshire Post*, 10 June, 1949.
'Not losing money on an ageing player': *Rugby Leaguer*, 2 April, 1953.
'Lionel Francis arrived in Belize City': O. Nigel Bolland, *Colonialism
    and Resistance in Belize, Second Edition* (University of West Indies
    Press, Kingston, 2003) 180.
'In 1921 he met Marcus Garvey': 'Marcus Garvey and the UNIA
    in British Honduras' Amandala, 16 September, 1994, at https://
    amandala.com.bz/news/marcus-garvey-and-the-unia-in-british
    -honduras, accessed 6 March 2022.

'This was not the end of the matter': Peter Ashdown, 'Marcus Garvey, the UNIA and the Black Cause in British Honduras, 1914–49', *Journal of Caribbean History* (1981) 15.

'The former miner from Brynmawr': The fullest accounts of the Morter dispute are in *Pittsburgh Courier*, 13 August, 1932 and *New York Age*, 27 August, 1932.

'She threw in her lot with Lionel': *New York Age*, 20 August, 1932.

'He was accused of unspecified "Conduct unbecoming"': *Pittsburgh Courier*, 19 May, 1934.

'Crazy like a fox with his eye on the Belize legacy': *New York Age*, 14 April, 1934.

'One person, one vote': Bolland, *Colonialism and Resistance*, 176; *Colonial Reports: British Honduras 1949* (HMSO, 1949) 5.

'Montego Bay conference': *Plain Dealer* (Kansas City), 12 September, 1947.

'His political power was waning': Larry Vernon, 'A history of political parties in Belize' in Lita Hunter Krohn et al., *Readings in Belize History* (National Institute of Culture and History, Belize, 1987) 239–55.

'Tremendous services to his fellow men': *Daily Clarion*, 10 and 11 May, 1961.

CHAPTER FIVE

'What are the basic things a coach requires?': Roy Francis interviewed in *The Mighty Bears, The History of North Sydney Rugby League from 1960 to 1970*, VHS video, Sydney 2002.

'A revolution could take place': George Dangerfield, *The Strange Death of Liberal England: 1910–1914* (Transaction Publishers, London, 1935) 208.

'When the season ended in April': *Hull Daily Mail*, 14 November, 1949 and 10 February, 1950.

'The directors said no': *Hull Daily Mail*, 8 and 10 April, 1950.

'Famously known as the "Blue Union"': Keith Sinclair, *How the Blue Union came to Hull Docks* (Hull, 1995).

'Heavy defeat at Dewsbury': *Hull Daily Mail*, 19 April, 1950.

'Roy was installed as the new club captain': *Hull Daily Mail*, 29 July, 1950.

'He began pre-season training in July': *Hull Daily Mail*, 11 September, 1951.

'When his playing days were over': *Hull Daily Mail*, 27 February, 1951.

'Local physiotherapist Jack Murray': *Hull Daily Mail*, 4 July, 1950.

'Prospects this season were bright': *Hull Daily Mail*, 8 August, 1951.

'Another derby win against Hull KR': *Hull Daily Mail*, 9 January, 1952;
    20 August, 1951; 10 September, 1951; 27 December, 1951; 12 April,
    1952.

'Friendly, but hardly progressive': *Hull Daily Mail*, 26 August, 1961.

'Confidence would grow': *Hull Daily Mail*, 11 September, 1951.

'The dearly beloved service tradition': *Hull Daily Mail*, 1 November, 1952.

'You're going to be a bloody fast hooker': *Hull Daily Mail*, 13 October,
    1962.

'I train my forwards like backs': *Hull Daily Mail*, 23 April, 1956.

'Survey of 76 football club managers': Neil Carter, *The Football Manager:
    A History* (Routledge, Abingdon-on-Thames, 2006) 60–61 and 71.

'The directors invariably voted for their coach's choice': *Hull Daily Mail*,
    22 September, 1962.

'It would be fatal': *Hull Daily Mail*, 7 February, 1952.

'Football is his first love': *Hull Daily Mail*, 10 August, 1957.

'Exactly the same': Roy Francis interviewed in *The Mighty Bears, The
    History of North Sydney Rugby League from 1960 to 1970*, VHS video,
    Sydney 2002.

'And so is the pitch!': *Hull Daily Mail*, 2 October, 1952.

CHAPTER SIX

'The other was me': *Hull Daily Mail*, 24 March, 1962.

'Coloured seamen now resident': *Hull Daily Mail*, 21 June, 1920.

'He never played in York's first team': His arrival (but not his words to
    Roy) was described in the *Hull Daily Mail*, 10 October, 1957.

'Ralph made a try-scoring debut': I am grateful to Bill Dalton for the
    statistics of Ralph Meheux's career.

'At least five black families were attacked': Jacqueline Jenkinson, *Black
    1919: Riots, Racism and Resistance* (Liverpool University Press,
    Liverpool, 2008) 206–8.

'His skin colour made him stand out more': Trevor Gibbons, *The Glory
    of Their Times: Crossing the Colour Line in Rugby League* (Vertical
    Editions, Skipton, 2003) 41.

'I could feel it in the air': Charlie Williams, *Ee – I've Had Some Laughs*
    (Wolfe Publishing Ltd., London, 1973) 38.

'Racism "is rather like flu"': *Sunday Telegraph* (Sydney), 11 April, 1971.

'Racialism, discrimination, whatever you like to call it': *Sunday Telegraph* (Sydney), 11 April, 1971.

'Cec Thompson also recalled the pain': Cec Thompson, *Born on the Wrong Side* (The Pentland Press, Bishop Auckland, 1995) 44.

'Roy Francis had every reason to complain': *Rugby Leaguer*, 28 August, 1964.

'They are trying to get under your skin': Oddy, *True Professional*, 126, 212.

'Roy was granted a licence': *Hull Daily Mail*, 7 February, 1956.

'A 16-year-old white girl': *Hull Daily Mail*, 7 May, 1959.

'Looking for his pregnant wife Joan': Robert Gate, *Billy Boston: Rugby League Footballer* (London League Publications Ltd., London, 2009) 62–3.

'We have no colour bar': *Rugby League Gazette*, 15 March, 1957.

'The selectors must be racists': Cec Thompson, *Born on the Wrong Side* (The Pentland Press, Bishop Auckland, 1995) 29.

'The open-style classical handling': *Hull Daily Mail*, 19 May, 1958.

'Teenage KR fan Dave Gotts': *Hull Daily Mail*, 7 and 9 May, 1959.

'We still have a few aces up our sleeves': *Hull Daily Mail*, 12 May, 1960.

'When Miles pointed to his name on the billboards': Miles Davis with Quincy Troupe, *Miles: The Autobiography* (Simon & Schuster, New York, 1989) 237–9.

'Liberated from this internal warfare': James Baldwin, *Notes of a Native Son* (Beacon Press, London, 2012) 169.

'Medical research in London as early as 1965': Ari Kiev, 'Psychiatric Morbidity of West Indian Immigrants in an Urban Group Practice', *British Journal of Psychiatry* (1965) 111: 55; Rebecca Pinto, Mark Ashworth and Roger Jones, 'Schizophrenia in black Caribbeans living in the UK: an exploration of underlying causes of the high incidence rate', *British Journal of General Practice* (2008) 58:551: 429.

'Ernie Hardaker denied any such thing': *Hull Daily Mail*, 5 and 6 May, 1962.

'He had decided on a complete shutdown': *Hull Daily Mail*, 6 June, 1963.

CHAPTER SEVEN

'The final act is down to you': Roy Francis quoted in Bev Risman, *Both Sides of the Fence* (Scratching Shed Publishing Ltd., Leeds, 2016) 26.

'An excess of kicking': Leeds Cricket, Football and Athletics Club, Football Committee minutes, 28 November, 1921. *West Yorkshire Archives*, WYL/2345/1/1.

'He had to buy some time': Phil Caplan, *Shoey the Lionheart: The Mick Shoebottom Story* (The History Press, Cheltenham, 2004) 40.

'I suppose it was a bit awkward': Ken Thornett interviewed by Ian Warden in the Sport Oral History Project: https://nla.gov.au/nla.obj -222002264/listen/0-5673, accessed 11 November, 2023.

'I was nowhere near his required fitness levels': Bev Risman, *Both Sides of the Fence* (Scratching Shed Publishing Ltd., Leeds, 2016) 121.

'Our only instructions were to play': Phil Caplan, *Shoey the Lionheart* (The History Press, Cheltenham, 2004) 61.

'In World War Two, black American GIs': Graham Smith, *When John Bull Met Jim Crow: Black American Soldiers in WW2 Britain* (I. B. Tauris London, 1987) 123–9.

'Looking back on the 1950s': Peter Read, *Charles Perkins: A Biography* (Viking, New York City, 1990) 61.

'I'm not dancing with you': Charlie Williams, *Ee – I've Had Some Laughs* (Wolfe Publishing Ltd., London, 1973) 56.

'Mobility in the forwards': *Rugby League News* (Sydney), 24 August, 1968.

'It all clicked': Phil Caplan, *Shoey the Lionheart* (The History Press, Cheltenham, 2004) 67

'Perfection on a football field': Caplan, *Shoey the Lionheart*, 67.

'You are all good enough': Bev Risman, *Both Sides of the Fence* (Scratching Shed Publishing Ltd., Leeds, 2016) 126.

'Who's this load of vagabonds?': David Hinchliffe, *They Walked on Water: The Untold Story of Wembley 1968* (Scratching Shed Publishing Ltd., Leeds, 2013) 158.

CHAPTER EIGHT

'I'm no Messiah': Roy Francis in *Rugby League World* (Sydney), April 1969.

'I have seen all the Leeds teams': *Rugby League News*, 13 March, 1969.

'All I wanted from the Leeds board': *Rugby Leaguer*, 13 April, 1989.

'We are the masters here': As told to star player Jim Bacon in Leeds Cricket, Football & Athletics Club, Football Committee minutes, 23 January, 1922. *West Yorkshire Archives*, WYL/2345/1/1.

'The situation was compounded': Andrew Moore, *The Mighty Bears: A Social History of North Sydney Rugby League* (MacMillan, Sydney, 1996) 220.

'He is working on the players' minds': *Rugby League News*, 23 June, 1968.

'Roy made a huge impression': Brian Norton interviewed in *The Mighty Bears, The History of North Sydney Rugby League from 1960 to 1970*, VHS video, Sydney 2002.

'The highest paid personality': *Rugby League News*, 19 August, 1968.

'I have decided to accept the offer': *Rugby Leaguer*, 27 September, 1968.

'The whole unprofessional attitude': Andrew Moore, *The Mighty Bears! A Social History of North Sydney Rugby League* (MacMillan, Sydney, 1996) 255.

'The portrait of the great West Indian cricketer': See www.poheritage.com, online exhibit 'Canberra, A Design Classic', accessed 4 May, 2023.

'I expect a lot from you': *Sydney Morning Herald*, 5 February, 1969.

'Francis Magic inspires Norths': *Rugby League World* (Sydney), April 1969.

'Making the baby-sitting offer': *Rugby League World* (Sydney), April 1969.

'To be born with this': *Sun-Herald* (Sydney), 19 April, 1970.

'An exercise in method acting': *Rugby League Week*, 25 April, 1970.

'Roy's half-time talks weren't rousing enough': Andrew Moore, *The Mighty Bears! A Social History of North Sydney Rugby League* (MacMillan, Sydney, 1996) 22.

'They were over-ambitious': *Rugby League Week*, Summer Special, 1986.

'I don't think Roy managed to continue': Denis Cubis interviewed in *The Mighty Bears, The History of North Sydney Rugby League from 1960 to 1970*, VHS video, Sydney 2002.

'Whether we like it or not': *Sydney Morning Herald*, 16 December, 1970.

'Casey was discriminating against him': Frank Hyde, *Straight Between the Posts* (Sydney, 1995) 225.

'When Charlie Williams accepted a contract': Charlie Williams, *Ee – I've Had Some Laughs* (Wolfe Publishing Ltd., London, 1973) 88.

'Equal rights to citizenship': Matthew Jordan (2018) 'Not on Your Life': Cabinet and Liberalisation of the White Australia Policy, 1964–67, *Journal of Imperial and Commonwealth History*, 46:1.

'"Whites-only policy" until the 1970s': Gwenda Tavan (2012) 'Fractured Families': The Jan Allen Controversy and Australia-British Relations, 1970–72, *Journal of Imperial and Commonwealth History*, 40:4

'A great artist': *Sydney Morning Herald*, 17 March, 1971.

'The property of Mr Roy Francis': *Sydney Morning Herald*, 31 March, 1971.

'He would have got them the premiership': Brian Norton interviewed in *The Mighty Bears, The History of North Sydney Rugby League from 1960 to 1970*, VHS video, Sydney 2002.

'The main thing that caused me to leave': *Rugby League Week*, Summer Special, 1986.

'The American writer James Baldwin': James Baldwin, *Notes of a Native Son* (Beacon Press, Boston, 2012) 94.

'You are coloured, you see, Mr Francis': *Rugby League Week*, Summer Special, 1986.

CHAPTER NINE

'Rugby that not only brought entertainment': Leeds RL Supporters' Club Handbook 1974–75 season, 11.

'Guests wore formal evening wear': *Hull Daily Mail*, 18 December, 1971.

'Roy's vast experience': *Hull Daily Mail*, 12 February, 1971.

'When you finish in Australia': *Hull Daily Mail*, 6 May, 1972.

'We must not penny-pinch': *Hull Daily Mail*, 26 August, 1972.

'Roy Francis is back in his old job': *Yorkshire Evening Post*, 28 May, 1974.

'It offered me the opportunity': Leeds RL Supporters' Club Handbook 1974–75 season, 11.

'When I joined Leeds in 1963': *Huddersfield Daily Examiner*, 19 May, 1975.

'Now I know I can turn it on again': *Manchester Evening News*, 26 April, 1975.

'If Saturday's display is a fair indication of what is in store': *Huddersfield Daily Examiner*, 19 May, 1975.

'My contract ends on May 31': *Yorkshire Evening Post*, 22 May, 1975.

'In my case you'll need a calendar': Peter Lush, *Ahead of His Time: Roy Francis and Rugby League* (London League Publications Ltd., London, 2022) 165.

'Entertainment and winning are not incompatible': Robert Gate, *Gone North* (R. E. Gate, Ripponden, 1986) 53.

CHAPTER TEN

'I loved Roy': Johnny Whiteley interview, 9 August, 2021.

'Bloody hell, everyone will be saying we're playing Roy Francis rugby!': Peter Roe interview, 26 February, 2024.

'It was not enough to dream': Roy Francis, as recounted by many interviewees.

Index